COMPETITION MONOLOGUES II

49 Contemporary Speeches for
Young Actors from the
Best Professionally Produced
American Plays

Edited and with an Acting Introduction by
Roger Ellis

UNIVERSITY
PRESS OF
AMERICA

Copyright © 1989 by

University Press of America®, Inc.

4720 Boston Way
Lanham, MD 20706

Library of Congress Cataloging-in-Publication Data

Competition monologues II : 49 contemporary speeches for young actors from
the best professionally produced American plays / edited and with an
acting introduction by Roger Ellis.
p.   cm.
Bibliography: p.
1. Acting—Auditions.   2. Monologues.   3. American drama—20th century.
I. Ellis, Roger, 1943 May 18–
PN2080.C644   1989   812'.045'08—dc19   89–5675 CIP

ISBN 0–8191–7439–4 (alk. paper)
ISBN 0–8191–7440–8 (pbk.: alk. paper)

All University Press of America books are produced on acid-free paper.
The paper used in this publication meets the minimum requirements of
American National Standard for Information Sciences—Permanence of Paper
for Printed Library Materials, ANSI Z39.48–1984.

For Jeremy, Kady, and Zan

A C K N O W L E D G M E N T S

Among the many groups and individuals who have given
me assistance over the years in compiling the material
for this book and in seeing it through the publication
pro-cess, there are several who deserve special thanks
for their much needed efforts. The Research and Development Committee and the School of Communications at
Grand Valley State University were instrumental in covering the costs of travel and in making arrangements
with the authors for the use of their material. All
of the playwrights whose work is included here were
very generous in granting me permission to use the ex-
tracts from their plays. Mr. Arthur Ballet of the
American Conservatory Theatre and Mr. David Carpenter
of the Mark Taper Forum were very helpful in helping
me locate scripts and authors in their new scripts
collections. Finally, I must also acknowledge the
kindness of numerous agents who sent me scripts for
perusal, and the efforts of many young actors whose
performances helped me to select and to shape the
monologues for inclusion.

C O N T E N T S

Preface to the Second Volume

This second volume of <u>Competition</u> <u>Monologues</u> is, like the first volume, designed specifically for young actors 18-28 years old. The inclusions are again drawn from American plays produced by professional regional theatres across the nation during the past few years. Because of this the scripts, with few exceptions, cannot be readily found in published form, and the monologues are therefore infrequently performed and highly original.

In addition to the joy of discovering this body of good monologue material and bringing it to the attention of actors and coaches, I've also found great pleasure in becoming acquainted with the large number of vital, well-written plays from which the selections have been drawn. As a result of suggestions from numerous coaches and drama teachers across the nation who have used the first volume in their classes and workshops, I've tried to include longer selections in this second volume. Hopefully this will help the general reader and the theatre practitioner to gain an understanding of the range and quality of solid dramatic writing which characterizes the contemporary American theatre, and which is too infrequently produced on our stages. Additionally, it will make it possible for acting teachers to use the selections as longer exercises in their general acting and theatre performance classes.

Finally, the reference section in "Appendix B" has been completely updated to reflect the wealth of material which has recently appeared in the monologue and auditioning field. My criteria for including certain works and omitting others is based partly upon the availability in print of these books and anthologies, and also upon my own estimation of the value and uniqueness of these works in the field.

Complete copies of the scripts from which the selections have been taken are readily available from the agents and authors listed in the "Credits" section, whose addresses are current at the time of publication. I share with them the hope that my anthology will not only help many actors to find good material for auditioning and class work, but will also encourage directors and producers to locate good original plays which certainly deserve more productions than they've had so far.

INTRODUCTION: To the Actor

Actors and Monologues

I've always felt that one of the worst burdens imposed on actors today is the demand that they audition with monologues. The monologue is now enshrined as part of the actor's equipment, just as essential as a resume, a union card, or an eight-by-ten glossy. Students must perform them for scholarship and entrance competitions, stock performers must run them by producers in thirty-to-sixty-second fragments at massive cattle calls, while other professionals must often deliver them to overworked and unsympathetic casting directors in offices or rehearsal halls or unfamiliar theatre stages.

Suddenly, that is, this administrative convenience of the dramatic monologue has become elevated to the status of the sink-or-swim entrance requirement (with devastating built-in judgments) for finding work in plays and often in the media. It is, after all, only an administrative convenience that directors use monologues at all. It would be totally unrealistic and impractical to expect every actor to bring along a friend for each audition in order to perform in a two-character scene. And so the monologue is used instead as a convenient device for looking closely at actors when casting plays.

The problem is that every one of us--directors, actors, coaches, producers--frequently place too much weight upon this solo performance, or mistake its value in a casting situation. Actors, for example, often feel they must provide the character which is being sought (as if they're expected to read the auditors' minds); or they must "blow the auditors out of the room" with their performances in order to get noticed; or they feel they should demonstrate as much "technique" as possible in the monologue so the director will know they're skilled and trained.

On the other side of the table casting people most frequently fall into the trap of expecting these kinds of monologue performances and of accepting them as final. Instead of looking for actors who can develop a role, auditors tend to look for "type," for finished products. There is no time. The "right" person is out there. The pressure of the casting situation often prods directors and actors to rely overmuch upon the monologue as the main indicator of "who is the right character" to play the role.

All of these confusions--and more--muddy the waters of our casting situations, especially for actors. Not knowing exactly what the directors are looking for, even if you've read the script, you're left with a host of contradictory choices in selecting and performing your monologue. Here are a few that have always plagued me:

"Are they looking for the traditional character, the straight character? Do they want the correct interpretation of the speech at this particular moment of the play?"

"Can I get some inside information on what the directors are looking for in order to shape my performance better?"

"Are they looking for my potential as an actor, regardless of the monologue I choose? or the way I choose to interpret it?"

"Should I select a monologue from the play being cast? If I do, will I run up against the director's fixed notion of whom he or she wants for the part?"

"Will the directors be comparing me with the actors they've seen in this role before? or earlier today? Should I therefore use a totally original monologue? Or do something offbeat?"

"Do I need to score an impression with something bold and physical, or something written with fireworks in order to earn a callback?"

"Does this monologue really show the range of my abilities? Is it appropriate for the part (whatever it is)?"

It's almost as though you feel yourself part of some cookie-cutter process (mold-ville Hollywood gone berserk) frantically caught up in the casting maze, trying to outguess the auditors as you decide which cartoon character they're looking for and which you're going to play.

But alas! The monologue is here to stay and we all learn to live with it, and to deal with it as another feature of doing business in this business we love. Yet despite all this confusion about monologue auditions, there is much that can be done to improve your performance of them in competitive situations.

Monologue workshops are offered in many cities, mainly by professional theatres. But there are few handbooks on the subject despite the fact that directors and coaches are pretty much in agreement of what goes into a good monologue audition. I'll be covering those points in the coming pages but before we get into that, there is one fundamental point I want to clarify: a monologue can and should only demonstrate an actor's <u>potential</u> for a role.

Yes, of course, the auditors are looking for the "right" actor to come along; but actors always make a big mistake by thinking the monologue can supply that magical pre-fabbed "character" who will fill the director's bill. Never aim at "character" in your monologue, aim only at honest responses to the dramatic situation. You can never know what exactly a director will be seeking, or what will turn a director off. So it's useless to try and it's a mistake to think of substituting a posture, an attitude, or a "character" for the emotional truth you've created and rehearsed.

Of course there are always directors who lack the time or the ability to look at an auditionee carefully. Frequently they're just trying to save themselves rehearsal work by finding someone ready-made. These kinds of directors lack confidence in their ability to coach an actor through rehearsals in order to develop a character. We must suffer such people--and they are numerous, believe me, especially in the media--because they give us work. If you're lucky enough to be the "type" they're looking for, well and good. But don't try to stuff your original self into some preconceived mold for the sake of a director who thinks he or she knows exactly what's called for. Most successful actors in auditions have shown directors dimensions to the role they never conceived of before-hand, and directors who deny this are most often rewarded with an opening night performance hardly different from the audition.

When an actor "goes for type" in this way, he or she has abandoned the one thing which can make the audition performance absolutely unique, special, and authentic: his or her own personality. Instead, the actor is left only with a simplification, a reduction of the role, an abstract idea which is supposed to fit the mold.   You cannot play an abstraction with any degree of interest, you must respond in truthful ways to the emotional circumstances in which the character finds himself or herself. That is what acting is all about--not living up to the expectations of a director, teacher, or agent.

The following suggestions for preparing monologues are all based on this belief that a good monologue audition, like any good acting performance, is never forgotten. Though you may not be "right" for this particular play or film, you will certainly score a strong impression in the auditors' memories. Producers and directors have told me this many times, and they've also stressed how quickly they eliminate and forget actors who are "acting all over the place" in monologue auditions, as though "technique" or "character" were theatrically interesting. They are not, and I know I'm not the only actor who's received a call months after I've been turned down for one role-- only to learn that the director remembered my acting and called me back to read for another part he was casting somewhere else.

For this reason I make my students in monologue classes refer to <u>themselves</u> in the situation and not to "the character." The temptation to throw up and hide behind a character is always deadly. Actors must learn instead to embody the character and experience the dramatic situation as fully as possible.

So in the suggestions which follow, remember always to place yourself in the circumstances of the role and avoid as much as possible distancing yourself from it, intellectually or emotionally. Avoid analyzing or explaining your monologue in terms like: "My character is . . ." or "My character feels . . . ." Always use yourself: "I am" or "I feel." As the great Stanislavski said about this "magic if" of acting: "Remove yourself from the plane of acting and place yourself instead on the plane of your own human emotions."

Monologues, then, must at all times be a vehicle for revealing yourself, <u>your</u> responses in the character's situation. If the casting people are looking for a strong "type," you can never know just what that means to them.   It's silly to worry about it because you'll either fit the type or you won't. What can and will interest them at all times is authentic, dynamic, and impassioned acting, and a stereotype can never be

5

as authentic as <u>your</u> <u>own</u> deeply-felt emotional life.

So have enough confidence in yourself to respond with all the richness and truth of a human being's emotional and intellectual life to the dramatic problems that the monologue presents, instead of acting what you <u>think</u> the auditors want to see. Your personalization of the dramatic material will always reveal a more interesting and compelling actor than any lifeless character-type is likely to produce. It's the necessary first step on the path leading to a successful monologue performance.

Selecting Monologues

I've called this anthology "competition" monologues because all the pieces I've selected are specifically suited to the competitive situation of auditioning. This sets the collection apart from other monologue anthologies on the market which are little more than collections of long speeches taken from plays. Although these monologue books are frequently an actor's first step in finding material to use for auditions, it's important to remember that most of them are assembled by people who have no particular skill or experience in auditioning as actors, directors, or coaches. Hence, they often lack those special features which distinguish speeches in plays from monologues that are well-suited to auditioning.

"What are those special features? What are the drawbacks of monologues that are simply lifted more or less verbatim from scripts? One of them is the fact that a character in a play who speaks at length in a monologue might simply be "talking to himself," calmly going over some of the events of the plot or making observations about other characters. Also, many speeches with strong emotions usually occur at a point where the performance has already gained some momentum prior to the character's situation of finding himself or herself alone at the moment. Finally, many speeches you'll find in plays often discuss subjects which are nostalgic and reminiscent for the character.

None of these qualities will help you in an audition. A monologue aimed at commenting upon or recounting the plot of a play is likely to be useless and uninteresting to directors casting a different play. And even if those circumstances do yield strong emotional responses in the speech, it often takes awhile

6

to build up to them. In an audition you don't have that time to "work into" your piece, to build up emotional momentum as a play can do in performance. Your monologue must be vital and compelling from the outset, since the directors are usually listening only for the first fifteen seconds. And finally, nostalgic and reminiscent monologues simply lack the emotional energy you need to propel yourself onstage for a strong audition.

Most speeches taken verbatim from plays work well in the context of that play's production, but not all of them are specifically aimed at presenting a human being grappling with important problems, and in need of communicating that experience to someone here-and-now. This is the main thing that makes a good audition piece.

The best monologues I've witnessed (acting abilities aside) have been those pieced-together from a two-person or three-person scene. Here the character is already involved with a strong give-and-take of ideas with others, struggling for communication and victory in getting what he or she wants. With the other character edited-out of the scene, the auditionee was able to patch together a single monologue from bits and pieces of dialogue.

With this kind of material you give the auditors a chance to see a much wider range of your talent as you develop from beginning to end in the scene. You use the other character's lines as a springboard, as your motivation for different reactions, different obstacles to encounter, new "events" which occur in the monologue and which force you to play constantly changing actions in response to them. I bring this up to stress the fact that there must always be other characters onstage with you, characters with whom you have a strong relationship as you deliver the speech to them.

Not all actors are good playwrights, however. Editing together a series of shorter speeches into a single consistent situation with a beginning-middle-end is not easy to do. And writing your own monologue is always deadly (unless you're as good a writer as Lanford Wilson, Sam Shepard, Wendy Wasserstein and others). Nor are actors familiar with a wide range of recent scripts to choose from, especially scripts containing characters within the age range of young performers. Perhaps for this reason alone, monologue anthologies are handy, popular choices for actors seeking auditioning material. But you will find that all the pieces included here possess that fundamental quality of a good audition which I just mentioned: they aim at presenting a character grappling with problems which he or she considers vitally important, and who also feels a strong need to communicate that experience to someone else.

Some of these monologues have been taken intact from plays, others have been pieced together from a series of shorter speeches with the lines of the other characters edited-out. What is important is that you concentrate upon that need to communicate in a relationship even though you're the only actor onstage. It is relationship which underlies every bit of acting you will ever do, and it must form the basis of single-character speeches just as it lies at the heart of multiple-character scenes.

Devising the Vis-a-Vis

"Vis-a-vis" is the technical term for the other (imaginary) character to whom you're speaking. Michael Shurtleff, America's most famous acting coach, recommends that you "bring a friend onstage with you so it won't seem as lonely" for you up there during your monologue. What he means is that you must have someone you're trying to influence during the monologue for it to work as it should. Without this other character onstage resisting you, attacking you, rejecting you, or even ignoring you, then your performance will always tend to be limp and flaccid, lifeless and unfocussed.

Now it's not always possible to know who this listener actually is. Some of your monologues, of course, have probably been taken from plays where the listener(s) are fairly well defined. For example, Katherina's famous speech at the end of Shakespeare's Taming of the Shrew where she is plainly speaking to the wedding guests. But other situations may not be as familiar to you. The monologues in this book, for example, are all taken from recent plays which might be difficult, and in many cases impossible, for you to find and read.

It isn't necessary, however, to read the whole script in order to do an excellent monologue, any more than it's necessary to read the entire play to do a good cold reading. The script will, of course, always give you a better idea of the background; but unless you're asked to do a specific speech for the audition, then there is no reason to worry about the whole play beforehand. You should not feel at a disadvantage because of this. Instead, familiarize yourself with the given circumstances found in the speech itself (a process of close reading and observation), and then add items from your own personal experience which are analogous to those of the character (a process of improvisation and substitution).

You'll find that most monologues give _some_ indication of who the listener is. But this kind of given circumstance is usually only minimal, and in any case it's not your own. The given vis-a-vis is another character in the play, but like any acting performance you must add your own personal belief to the vis-a-vis in order to give that person life and make him or her work for you in the audition.

This is done by means of the acting method called "substitution," whereby you substitute real people, experiences, emotions and the like from your own background for those in the play. It helps you to identify more easily with the role and the play's circumstances. But whether you completely _invent_ your vis-a-vis and the reasons why you're speaking to that person, or whether you _deduce_ those things from the monologue itself, _what matters is your commitment to the goal you're trying to accomplish with the speech, what you're trying to do to the other character._ The casting folks will never know what personal stimuli you're using to energize the speech. They'll only be concerned with the intensity and believability of your acting. And this is why the proper choice of a vis-a-vis can be enormously helpful in performance.

To begin with, you should pick an imaginary listener who is unsympathetic to your character's needs and desires. This will automatically ensure that there is conflict in the scene, and will force you to fight strongly for what you want. Stop for a moment and think of some of the most famous monologues and soliloquies ever written--those from Jonson, Moliere, or Shakespeare. Conflict is always up front in those speeches.

Although they appear to be alone, no character is ever truly alone onstage. Hamlet, for example, is really talking "to" and "about" his father (who re-

9

peatedly whips Hamlet on to avenge his murder), his mother (who has cheapened herself by marrying Claudius), his stepfather (a murderer who has stolen Hamlet's inheritance), and his fiancee Ophelia (who insists on loving him despite his madness). His famous soliloquies are not decorative literary speculations for the audience's edification, but vital arguments--pro and con--about the need to take extreme action. Hamlet's speeches may be arguments "with himself" onstage, but they're also arguments with these other characters (many of whom he actually addresses in the lines of the soliloquy). This is what makes them vital, compelling to listen to, and dramatic.

You must create this same kind of demanding vis-a-vis for yourself. Use someone from your own life because then you can see that person concretely in your imagination. Place him or her downstage of you (so you'll always be "open" to the directors), and visualize specific reactions of that person to the words you're saying. Imagine him or her getting up to leave, shrugging the shoulders, voicing a protest, shock, or disbelief at what you're saying. Use those reactions to reinforce your delivery of the words, your changes in mood, your different tactics to get that person to do what you want. Create a compelling relationship with your vis-a-vis and you'll add tremendous vitality to your monologue.

Secondly, the other character should be someone who is _important_ to you, whose opinions and actions you need and respect. This person can be an enemy (Hamlet's Claudius is a "bloody, bawdy, damnable villain"), or a friend or relative (Hamlet's Ophelia is someone he loves but whom he is desperately trying to offend and reject). Frequently the best listeners are those like Ophelia with whom you have a love-hate relationship. This will always make a monologue performance more rich, mysterious, and unpredictable. No matter that your concerns aren't as politically weighty as those of Hamlet, nor that your listeners aren't kings, queens, murderers, and the like. All that matters in the audition is that you commit yourself absolutely to winning over your vis-a-vis, just as Hamlet does in his situation.

If you make the stakes of the conflict high enough then your acting will automatically become more vigorous and interesting to the casting people. The vis-a-vis should therefore be a character who is capable of providing whatever it is that you need to turn your life around and win happiness. Your character's problem--your problem--is not something which can be overcome by mundane solutions which anyone can offer. Only this vis-a-vis can do it for you, only this dramatic encounter holds life or death importance for you. Which brings me to my next point: what do you want from your vis-a-vis?

Goals and Obstacles

Many coaches say that an ability to understand and to play goals and obstacles in a scene lies at the heart of good acting. An actor who knows--or who gives the audience the impression of knowing--what he or she wants in a scene, who speaks and moves purposefully, and who seems to be willing to engage in any conflict in order to achieve his or her purpose is an actor who will compel our attention and create a convincing character. Inventing goals for your character is one-half of the battle here. The other half is finding out what it is about your vis-a-vis that prevents you from achieving those goals and obstacles.

Your goal in the dramatic situation of the monologue is never single, it must always be multiple. In life we never get what we want without having to overcome many obstacles along the way: other drivers on the freeway, greedy ex-wives, domineering parents, uncommunicative lovers, unsympathetic bankers, and so many more. And in each encounter there will be a number of things we want from that other person. In fact, we often only discover them in he course of the encounter, because of the encounter.

Now this always happens in two-character scenes where the beats change as the scene develops, and remember that you're treating the monologue as a two-character scene for auditioning purposes. So in the speech you should look in the lines for what your character seeks and just what stands in his or her way. If it's not indicated in the text then you must invent and improvise your own. Then identify how your goals change in the monologue as your character's thoughts develop.

These different goals must always be clear to you moment by moment. You must attack each of them strongly when they occur in the speech for variety, contrast, and pace. Uta Hagen remarks that this is one of the most valuable things an actor can do in a mono-

11

logue: playing the pattern of actions which will give dramatic shape and development to the speech. At the same time, your goals should change as the other characters--the vis-a-vis--_force_ you by their reactions to change them.

So use your vis-a-vis in two ways here: as a person from whom you _need_ something vital for your own happiness, and as a person who continually _denies_ you this victory. This will intensify the performance by deepening the relationship between you. You will creeate and define that relationship by playing these patterns of goals and obstacles during the performance.

It is also important that you identify and phrase these goals in strong terms. Robert Cohen, a professional acting coach and director from California, recommends that actors use the idea of "winning a victory." This will help you to keep the stakes of the conflict important in your own mind. Aaron Frankel, the noted Broadway director, uses the phrase "an itch that you've just got to scratch." Michael Shurtleff calls it "what you're fighting for" because the word "fight" is all-important for your energy and dynamism during the audition. Jane Brody, Director of Chicago's Audition Centre, often uses the following terms in her classes: "This is a scene about me in a love relationship with the other person. What is the problem we're having?"

I think the word "love" can be extremely useful if you keep in mind that love means many things between people. The Romeo and Juliet kind of love is probably the most familiar to young actors, but it only describes one kind of relationship, and it isn't very commonly found in monologues. There is also the love of brother for sister, wife for ex-husband, parent for child, murderer for victim, friend for friend, therapist for patient, student for teacher, etc. Thus love means more than romantic affection: it can also signify respect, trust, support, friendship, dependency, comfort, cooperation, and other things. But by using the word "love" you automatically intensify and deepen the playing of all your feelings durring the monologue performance.

Very few dramatic monologues or scenes are written which deal with the happy fulfillment of one character's love for another. Even Romeo and Juliet, though their love is plainly strong and pure, must overcome a host of obstacles in order to win the love they feel for each other: bickering parents, social disapproval, mocking friends, and even scheduling problems which arise from finding suitable times and places for their lovemaking. They are continually involved with planning secretly, resisting the pressures from their parents, persuading Friar Lawrence, escaping jail, etc. In most plays it is the denial of love, from a variety of sources, which propels the action forward.

You must identify in your monologue what kind of love your character is seeking, and what denials he or she is encountering. Your vis-a-vis is the only person who can help you towards these goals, and you need that person here and now. Try to be very concrete about what you want your vis-a-vis to do, and what you're trying to do to that character at each and every moment in the monologue. Some workable choices in this respect might be "to manipulate," "to abuse," "to cause guilt," "to seduce," "to blame," "to get even," "to flatter," and so on. Reinforce these with two or three concrete physical activities for you to do onstage during the speech.

Always remember that the casting people will never know what these goals actually are; they'll only be attentive to the force of your acting, to the enerrgy with which you play the monologue's dramatic situation.

Getting Onstage

One final point, critical for an audition, needs to be mentioned here. Remember that acting in an audition will always differ from acting in a play or in a studio scene in that the audition performance requires vitality and urgency right from the outset. You must compel the auditors' attention, curiosity, and interest during the first few moments. Directors usually make crucial decisions about your abilities from the way you take the stage and introduce yourself even before you begin "acting." A cliche that is nonetheless true is that directors often reach a decision about you in the first fifteen seconds of the audition.

Most of the monologues in this anthology provide good strong acting choices right from the outset of the speech, and you must rehearse to play these strongly. Again, some monologues give clear indica-

tions of such choices in the lines, while others require that <u>you</u> invent your own circumstances not only
throughout the speech but especially at the beginning.

I can't say too much about this need to kick-off
your audition with energy and drive. Most actors already know that you must "get your best up front" and
"lead with your strengths" either on their resume or
in the audition. And many actors have their own methods for doing this in performance. Sometimes (rarely,
I think) the motivation for attacking strongly from
the outset is built into the speech itself, or in the
given circumstances of the play.   Obviously in the
performance of a whole play this sort of motivation is
part of the actor's consistent through-line, but in an
audition you lack this emotional momentum to bank
upon. You simply make your entrance, do your introduction to the directors, then--bang!--you're on.

You need more than just the given circumstances
of the play or the monologue in order to accomplish
this kickoff effectively. No matter how compelling
your character's situation may be in dramatic terms,
those terms are not your own--they are the play's.
What <u>you</u> need as an actor is something else, some
personal trigger for your emotional commitment and
belief which can propel you into the first moments
with little or no preparation.

Actors do this most frequently by using what
Stanislavski called "emotional memory." All of us have
a wealth of intense emotional experience in our past
lives. Often we repress such knowledge because it's
painful: memories of death or loss, the breakup of a
love relationship, an accident which occurred to you
or to a loved one. On the other hand we frequently do
call to mind the intense <u>positive</u> memories and feelings we have. Is there anyone who hasn't daydreamed
or "replayed scenarios" of those happy times in order
to imaginatively re-live them? Moments of victory in a
ballgame, the thrill and tingle of that first kiss
with someone special, the surprise and delight in re-
ceiving a long-awaited message or gift? Often we che-
rish such experiences in our waking fantasies for
years after they originally occurred; and invariably
they carry along with them many related <u>sensory</u> im-
pressions: the fragrance of his cologne, the chill of
the autumn air, the bright colors of the setting, and
so on. You need these kinds of vivid images in order
to energize the monologue from the opening moments.

You can evoke these feelings in yourself very easily by finding a key word or image which serves as an instant trigger for recalling the experience. In everyday life isn't this how it frequently happens? The sound of a familiar tune, a casual remark by someone, the discovery of some long-forgotten object in an old box--and suddenly we're plunged into the sadness or the fear or the ecstasy of remembrance. Indeed, it's often more intense in recollection (or so it seems) than it was at the time. Actors frequently do this in order to cry onstage, to register shock, or joy, or fear.

So once you've rehearsed other aspects of your monologues, look to add this kind of inciting action at the opening in order to be "on" from the very first. An unmistakable kiss of death in an audition is an actor taking forever to "get into character" before starting, while the directors lose interest and curiosity with each dismal second that passes. And then to have the actor slowly drift into the piece as he or she gradually works up excitement. By that time, of course, the auditors are usually sending out for coffee, leafing through their notes of prior auditionees, or fumbling under their seats for a dropped pencil. They let you continue, perhaps, out of courtesy or because something might eventually "happen" as you drone on in the background. But most of the time you're only just digging yourself out of the grave you created in the opening moments.

Most people who don't understand acting at all hold very different ideas about how their own emotions operate. In short, they're victims of their emotions. They don't believe that emotion can--or even should-- be turned on-and-off like a faucet because there's something arbitrary, dishonest, or phoney about that when they do it in "real" life. As an actor, however, you must be more in touch with and more in control of your emotional life than ordinary people. You understand that the emotional "truth" of a dramatic situation can be communicated to an audience by many methods, and often without your feeling anything in the performance (except perhaps for stage fright!). I'm often amazed after a performance when a spectator tells me that some moment was "so moving and believable" when in fact I was totally unmoved at the time it happened onstage; or when I _was_ acting my guts out and a spectator says that the moment rang false. Ah, the tricks and techniques we use in this business to create lies like truth!

So with this final suggestion to energize the opening moments of your monologue performance, look for those personal associations and key words or images that can trigger the strong feelings you need to get out onstage with focus and purposefulness. It's useful and necessary in <u>every</u> audition. And who knows? If your emotional memory contains an incident analogous or even identical to that of your character, then so much the better. It sometimes happens.

Good luck with the monologues that follow. And keep in mind that the prefatory remarks which accompany each are only <u>suggestions</u> for you. They're simply things to consider, handy departure points for the unique choices <u>you</u> should add in order to create a vital, compelling human relationship onstage with your vis-a-vis.

NOTES ON THE MONOLOGUES

1. Most of the monologues can be performed within a two-minute limit, and many are as short as one minute. Longer selections have been included for class or studio work, but these have been selected with an eye to their possibilities for cutting, should that be necessary. In this case, lines should be edited-out <u>internally</u> rather than by simply lopping off the necessary number of lines at the beginning or end.

2. Where the monologue specifically requires an actor of a particular ethnic background, this has been indicated. Most of the monologues, however, are suitable for performers of any ethnic background whatsoever.

3. The age range of the character indicated at the top of each selection is only a rough suggestion. The age of any dramatic character is not necessarily the same as the actor's age, since "range" means what an actor is physically and emotionally capable of playing with believability. You should therefore use your own judgment in deciding upon the actual age of the character, and whether the piece falls within your emotional range.

4. The designations "comic/serious/seriocomic" are

also suggestions and you should not feel absolutely constrained to adhere to these guidelines.

5. In preparing to rehearse these pieces, you should make three xerox copies of the selection. Set one aside for the final version, and use the other two to mark up as necessary for interpretation: pauses, stresses, pacing, inflection, etc. When you're satisfied with the approach to playing it, then reinforce what you've rehearsed by scoring the final xerox copy in the manner you've chosen. Keep it by you for reading over, since your marks on the sheet will help remind you of the technical points you've identified.

6. The terms "ladder" and "stepping stone" in referring to monologues are occasionally used in the prefatory notes. A ladder type speech is one which builds in emotional intensity more or less consistently from beginning to end (sometimes called a climactic speech). The stepping stone monologue creates emotional peaks at various points according to various stimuli during the speech. It's high point may sometimes occur at the end, but it cannot be effectively played as a straightforward gradual build in intensity. Learning how to identify and to play the high points in a speech effectively is the key here.

MONOLOGUES FOR WOMEN

CAUGHT, by Bernard M. Kahn

Madeleine--18   Female--Serious

The character's vis-a-vis in this piece is a married
man with whom Madeleine has become involved, and there
a number of places where the actor can visualize prob-
able reactions from her vis-a-vis as she is speaking.
The strength of the piece lies in the fact that Madeleine is torn between her love for David and the knowledge that their relationship is no good for her.

David, we've got some serious talking to do. And don't
tell me you have to go. I would've picked last night
but . . . I wanted us to be together . . . really together. Another week here or there is not going to do
it for me. Two and a half years have gone by and I
don't know where they went. I can't do this any more.
I'm sick of sneaking around . . . whispered phone
calls . . . broken dates . . . planned vacations
that never happen. I just don't feel good about what
we're doing, and what really bothers me is that I have
this feeling that you can go on like this forever.
When you leave me, you go back to your family. I've
got nobody. I spend most of my time waiting and wondering when I'll see you again. I'm lonely, David.
You asked me what I was going to do today . . . how
come you never ask me what I'm going to do at night?
You don't want to know . . . as long as I'm not with
another man. Right? You know what I'm getting mostly
out of this relationship? I'm becoming well-read. I'd
love to know what you think of when you walk out that

19

door. Am I still on your mind . . . or do you say to yourself, "That'll take care of her for a few days?" My girlfriend Barbara thinks I'm crazy. She says you'll never get a divorce. It's the old cake-and-eat-it-too syndrome. It means . . . that in all this time . . . I hardly know you. David, we're either in some dark restaurant or in bed. This is not what is called a normal courtship.

THE PROCESSORS, by Roberta Parry

Leslie--20s   Female--Comic

<u>One of this monologue's strongest features is that it can be delivered directly to the audience, like a sales presentation. The sexual innuendoes should not be overworked since they are very clear in the writing which builds surely and dynamically to a solid, humorous ending. Finally, no attempt should be made to cartoonize the character, in fact, Leslie can be effectively played as a very intelligent woman who knows exactly what she's communicating.</u>

Meet Willie. Willie Word Processor. I keep Willie right here in my bedroom, next to my bed, where I can talk to and touch him any time I want. He's such fun to fiddle with. I just <u>love</u> manipulating his little buttons, making him do exactly what I want. The best thing about Willie is he's always available, always plugged in, always ready to light up for me and come on line. We have such interesting interfaces, Willie

20

and I. He's so smart. He holds a bank of important information in that incredible memory of his. And he has a network of influential international connections. But he doesn't mind sharing his little secrets with me at all. I can always rely on him to tell me exactly what I want when I want it--not like some men I know. And he never tries to put me down or take over. He knows who's boss. He'd make a wonderful business partner. With Willie, you wouldn't need anyone else. The other thing I like about Willie is his strong, square, masculine lines. I shiver at the cold hardness of him against me and the soft humming he makes when I fill his drive. Now, I must admit I don't understand too well how Willie works, all those BIOS and buffers and K-bytes. But it doesn't seem to affect his baud rate or RAM. As long as I know how to turn him on and play his keyboard, he's ready to go up. Willie or Wontie? And Willie's always willing. Willie's a Wonder!

ONCE UPON A TIME, by Harry Hattyar

Roberta--28   Female--Comic

This comedy, an modern re-telling of the Cinderella story, contains a number of sparkling scenes. In this passage, the fairy godmother is bundling Cinderella

21

off to Prince Milton's ball. In fact at the opening
she makes a reference to call the laundry service
instead of staying home to do the housework! The piece
requires a comedy of manners approach by an actress
with "style." The character is very much a type of
modern socialite, and the monologue presents strong
acting challenges in the areas of language, movement,
and characterization.

Hello, darling. Listen, I don't want to waste time explaining things. I want you to go to Milton's ball tonight. I know: the laundry. Don't worry about it. And stop fidgeting. We'll get a five-hour laundry service to take care of it. Some have pick-up and delivery service, you know. Now listen carefully, darling. I've got you clothes, undies, everything in here. They'll fit you to perfection. I also ordered a cab which is waiting outside to take you to Milton's place. You just walk in, dazzle the hell out of the congregation, wrap Milton around your finger, and have a blazing good time. But you must be very careful to leave before the clock strikes midnight. Anything wrong with midnight? How old are you, darling? Nineteen . . . Well! Let's make it two a.m. then. We're not living in the middle ages, are we?. But be very careful to leave before the clock strikes two, and by no means must you tell anybody, but anybody, who you are and where you live. Let the bastards guess. Now, on your way. Get dressed and enjoy yourself. (ANGEL-
ICA exits. ROBERTA sighs with relief, as at a job

well <u>done.)</u> That should take care of it. It pisses me off the way they treat the poor girl. Oh, I wish I could see the expressions on their faces . . . What am I talking about? Am I a witch or not? I will!

SWEET TABLE AT THE RICHELIEU, by Ronald Ribman

Jeanine--28   Female--Serious

<u>This wonderfully lyrical piece presents a strong challenge for the actor to keep her energy up from the very outset. It is all too easy for the actor to lose urgency when delivering lines like these. The choice of a strong vis-a-vis is critical: it should be a listener whose opinions Jeanine greatly respects and whom she is desperately seeking to influence.</u>

I have hope . . . yes. Like your cricket rubbing its legs a final time in the lizard's mouth . . . I have that hope. I dream that. I fall asleep on the rusted and mildewed furniture in my backyard and I dream that all this universe is nothing but the breath of a <u>sleeping</u> giant. That every time he breathes out a hundred billion years go by, and every time he breathes in it all collapses into nothingness again. That if only I can hold on to my son long enough some puff of breath may bring him to me again. We are each other's dream. He dreams he is me sleeping in the sun dreaming I am him. And having gone around in a circle to which there is neither end nor answer given to any-

23

thing, I open my eyes in the office of my husband's lawyers, or on the stone platform of a bus stop in Sewickley, watching the blossoms of snow fall down, weighing down my lids, closing them again, till it seems I am lost in the middle of a dark wood, hearing only the sound of the distant sleigh of the Richelieu come to bear me away. Is that the best we can do, Signor Bottivici? Chirp our legs like crickets going

down the lizard's throat?

LEAVIN' JOE, by Sheila Ganz

Princess-18   Female--Comic

This young girl's paraphrase of Juliet's famous words to Romeo is a ladder-type of monologue where the character becomes increasingly more caught-up with her emotions as the speech progresses. The comedy should arise from her absolute belief in the feelings she's expressing--she isn't trying to be funny. A strong vis-a-vis for auditioning purposes might be the young boy playing Romeo.

Oh, Romeo, I wish that you were here this very moment, to relieve this desperate feeling I have. Why won't you come to me now? I implore you, I beseech you. You are my life, I could not live without you. You know that, don't you? I don't care if my family is so stupid, they won't let me see you. I will be your wife. And, your family is troubled the same way, but I don't

24

feel anger towards them, my love, because your mother bore you as some day I wish, I pray, I might bear your children. Will it ever come to pass? We live for the few moments we steal from each other. Why can't we sing under the sun together as we sing under the stars? I pray you do not keep me waiting much longer. I know it must be something urgent that keeps you, that you feel the same way as I. You did yesterday, did you not, my darling? My precious. Your eyes are the sky to me. It is only when I gaze at you that I feel complete. My hands tremble at the thought of you, my heart races. It is impossible to tell how much joy you give me when you smile at me. My world is lit like a giant Japanese lantern on a festival day. And, when you are not in my sight, my despair is almost over-whelming. I implore you to hurry to my side. For you to tell me again, how your heart throbs and pounds for me. For you to caress my hair and gently put your arms around me. I would nearly faint. I long to feel your breath on my ear and neck. The delicious goosebumps you create no other could ever compare. Hurry! I see the moon passing behind clouds that shimmer and drift showing you the path to my heart, to my arms. The stars shine so bright I know you must not be far. I'll make a wish for you to be by my side always. For us never to part. For the day to come, not far off, when the good friar will join us forever in holy marriage and no family will cut us apart. We will live and survive on each other's sweet breath, your lips and teeth biting in mine. My eyes closed to feel all the colors of rapture that no artist could ever paint. I know you grow near. We will feel our two bodies pressing against each other with the force of a passion this planet has never felt before. We will be one as we rock in each other's arms. Your manliness enveloped in me. The sweet tingling will be unbearable. Your hard muscles nearly crushing me in their tenderness and love and the burning need for your mouth to suck like some innocent babe I will rock to sleep in my arms.

ANKHST, by Clarinda Karpov

Judy--28   Female--Serious

This monologue is played most effectively when the actress uses her vis-a-vis strongly from beginning to end. Judy, a disciplined, professional archeologist is frustrated by the fact that all of her scientific training and experience fail to provide her with the answers she desperately seeks about a recent discovery she has made. She must explain to Alex--whom she has criticized earlier--why she is so passionately consumed by this quest for understanding. Only Alex can help her to find the answers she needs.

Do you think there's no passion without noise and

theatrics? Shall I try to explain to you mine? How I came to Egyptology? I killed a man. Just out of high school, I went to Israel to work on a kibbutz. Hostilities broke out in the neighborhood, and I became involved, remained involved for many months, and then--in a skirmish, I killed a man--a girl not out of her teens, and I killed a man. I was wounded myself, not critically, but it gave me time to think, in the hospital, stared at all the while by the face of the man I'd killed--who would have killed me. The first thing I saw was, I'd lost a year of life. I mean, I'd come to plant turnips in a cause I'd been raised to believe in, and I hadn't planted turnips in a long time. And I saw that the man I killed hadn't planted, or written poetry, or whatever he'd do, and never would. All my zealotry ebbed away. All our aspirations were one and as old as time. I saw no particular hope in the future, so I looked for it in the past. Not escapism, Alex: it was like prospecting. If I go far enough back, it may be like climbing a mountain, above the bank of clouds, to where you can see the unclouded dawn--before the choices were made that have chosen us. Marshalling all the resources of earth and time to face Armageddon. I give Egypt its image, and Egypt gives me the chance to know what made the man I killed. To understand the past for the sake of the

27

future. Can you see that? I dig for understanding, not treasures. And here we've found an extraordinary treasure masking, perhaps, a great truth, with no likelihood of our ever seeing its face.

MAJOR APPLIANCES, by Marc Handler

Manikin--20s   Male/Female--Comic

This monologue has a strong vis-a-vis: a crowd of enthusiastic listeners whose reactions the actor should visualize as concretely as possible. It also possesses several opportunities for the speaker to "change direction" with his or her appeals, so the selection develops swiftly and suddenly with numerous twists and turns. By all means the actor should avoid delivering the "speech" as a harangue with only one or two emotional colors.

Fellow manikins! The time has come for change! It is the humans who say, "Avoid the ways of the flesh." Yet who has avoided the ways of the flesh more than us?! And where has it gotten us!? They speak of original sin? What hypocrisy! They are the ones who persist in having genitals, not us! From sawdust you came, and to sawdust you shall return! Yet the Manikin God is ever-lasting! It is time to shed the pitiful clothing foisted upon you by these backward humans! Are you afraid of the cold? The heat? The wind? Do you need to vie for rank and status through your choice of clothing?

28

Are you ashamed of your manikin bodies? Afraid that
someone will see your genitals? Then take them off!
That's right! Take off your wretched human clothes and
stand naked before the Manikin God! Look at you!
You're beautiful! You are the ultimate hard
bodies! . . . But wait, I see one couple over there,
still clothed. And I'm sure we can all guess why. Come
up here--don't be afraid. Come on, we all understand--
for who among us has not himself been tempted. You are
among friends. Now go ahead, take off your clothes.
Just as I thought--you've painted genitals on yourselves! Don't laugh! This is serious! How many of us
have humiliated ourselves in this or some other pitiful manner because we allowed them to convince us that
they are superior? Think of the wonderful smoothness
God has put between our legs! Humans will never know
the incomparable ecstasy of rubbing smooth hard
crotches against one another. No, we are the superior
ones. We are the crown of creation. And it's time to
be proud of it! You womanikins must stop hiding beneath these paltry imitations of human hair! Be bold;
be bald! And glory in your baldness! Stomp those wigs
into the ground! That's it! Remember: god made manikin
in his own image! You must love yourselves as you are!
Now I know some of you are saying, "what about the
humans?" Well, what about the humans!? When they've

unleashed their hydrogen bombs and they're writhing in the death throes of radiation poisoning, what will <u>you</u> be doing? Laughing! Having a party! That's right! We who are immune to radiation and chemical toxicity, WE WILL INHERIT THE EARTH! Say it with me! "God is good! God is wood! God is good! God is wood! God is . . . ."

THIS ONE THING I DO, by Claire Braz-Valentine

Susan B. Anthony--20s   Female--Seriocomic

<u>This monologue must be played gently, in a stepping-
stone fashion, as the character presents us with an
honest explanation of who she is and what she wants
out of life. It has the advantage of working from an
historical base--Susan B. Anthony's actual achieve-
ments--which are familiar to most listeners, while
giving us the "inside" feelings of the historical
character.</u>

It's not that I want to be a man . . . but sometimes I wonder--you know, about people and their spirits. I sometimes wonder if spirits have gender. I mean, if I took my brain out and put it on the table and Bobby Gilbert, who lives down the street, took his brain out and put it on the table, would anyone be able to tell the difference? Whose was the boy's and whose was the girl's? That wouldn't work. <u>(Giggles.)</u> Bobby Gilbert is stupid. His brain would be much smaller. They could tell that way. But if women aren't allowed to go

30

to college . . . work in business . . . enter into politics . . . then how come I began to read when I was three years old? Would God be so unjust as to give me a mind to work with and then not let me use it? It's not that I want to be a man . . . but don't you think that would be crazy? And God's not crazy, but I would be if I'm not allowed to use my mind. It's not that I want to be a man . . . I want . . . to drive a carriage . . . . Oh yes, it's lovely to be picked up on Sundays by suitors and be taken for a drive, but . . . I would like . . . an excellent position in a fine firm. I would like to be able to walk into a bank. I would like to not wear a corset. It's not that I want to be a man . . . I want to be a person.

M. BUTTERFLY, by David Henry Hwang

Suzuki--20's   Female--Comic

This monologue is very straightforward, with the character speaking firmly and persuasively to her vis-a-vis, whom she believes has entered into a bad relationship with a foreigner, an American. The piece presents opportunities for an actress to add a variety of emotional colors to the main one of sarcasm.

Girl, he's a loser. What'd he ever give you? Nineteen cents and those ugly Day-Glo stockings? Look, it's

finished! Kaput! Done! And you should be glad! I
mean, the guy was a woofer! He tried before, you
know--before he met you, he went down to geisha central and plunked down his spare change in front of the
usual candidates--everyone else gagged! These are
hungry prostitutes, and they were not interested, get
the picture? Now, stop slathering when an American
ship sails in, and let's make some bucks--I mean, yen!
We are broke! Now, what about Yamadori? Hey, hey--
don't look away--the man is a prince--figuratively,
and, what's better, literally. He's rich, he's handsome, he says he'll die if you don't marry him--and
he's even willing to overlook the little fact that
you've been deflowered all over the place by a foreign
devil. What do you mean, "But he's Japanese?" What do
you think you are? You think you've been touched by
the whitey god? He was a sailor with dirty hands!

NIGHT BREATH, by Dennis Clontz

Two--28   Female--Serious

This thoughtful monologue has a strong narrative line
in the story of the miner. Although the tale does have
a definite beginning, middle and end, it does not
readily offer the actor any explosive "high points."
Thus it's well-suited to an actor who can invest the
narrative with special importance for the character.
Avoid the tendency to perform a quiet "memory piece"

which lacks energy, and instead play Two's puzzlement,
curiosity, and search for meaning in the story as she
is speaking.

Rosie, she was staying in a temporary way, before
coming to California, in this small mining town out
near Ajo. Weren't much there. Just a bunch of copper
miners cussing Arizona with talk of Alaska and gold.
Loud folk they were. Big talking, big dreaming, small
doing. All pretty much alike. Excepting this one--
fixing to go to Alaska like the rest, but not for
gold. Gonna get himself a snow bear, a giant one with
white fur all over. He ain't never seen no white bear,
so he figured it the most--special--thing on God's
created Earth. Lord, how he wanted that thing, that--
snow bear . . . . That miner. He was all the time
showing off this here steel trap he had to catch the
critter with. Rambling on and on 'bout that snow bear
like there was but one in the whole state of Alaska.
Specially drunk, whew, would his tongue spark fires!
Well, one drunk night, God knows what he was doing
with that trap, but it snapped on him. Got him in the
belly . . . And, ahh, he's in our room, down on his
knees, curled over that trap. Won't let nobody touch
him. Won't let them work the. trap for fear his insides will fall out if'n it opens up. And he gets
strange, you know. Confused 'bout things. Then, God
knows how, that man gets to his feet, holding on to

that trap, and he carries it with him out the door
into the street. And damn if he's not walking out of
town thinking he's on his way to Alaska . . . . Well.
He makes it `bout a quarter a mile before collapsing.
Rest of the night before dying. The whole time
thinking--believing--he's in Alaska. And, ahh, right
before the end, he thinks he has trapped a snow bear.
Seems like everybody got their own kind of snow bear
they're after.

MAJOR APPLIANCES, by Marc Handler

Punk--20s   Male/Female--Comic

This selection offers a wealth of interpretive possibilities for the actor. It can be zany and free-
form, it can parody the "standard" TV news style, it
can be smooth and syrupy, or hard-hitting and
"straight from the shoulder," etc. Two approaches,
however, should be avoided because they lack performance energy: the monotone or "punk" style suggested
by the character, and the colorless pseudo-objectivity
of the TV journalist-reporter.

Today's disease index: socially transmitted diseases
are up four and five eighths, radiation poisoning, up
ten and a quarter, skin cancer up one and a half as
scientists continue their attempts to recreate the
ozone layer. Uncontaminated bottled water can be pur-
chased in the northwest section of the city--be pre-

34

pared to wait. The east side is still off-limits due to toxic spills, and Crips have told the Mayor's office that they will permit Red Cross paramedics to enter the central city, but only if their gang leaders are allowed free passage through the metropolitan districts still held by city police. The stock market continued to plummet for the two hundred and fifty-fourth straight day this year as the exchange rate stabilized at eight thousand dollars to the yen. City officials have unveiled a new plan for relieving the gridlock claiming that before the end of the year vehicles will once again begin to move, at least in selected sectors of the city. This comes on the same day the state congress has proposed reopening schools for children, on a limited basis. And today's body count, down from yesterday at 114 lost in fly-by shootings, 12 killed by skyscraper snipers, 26 in hamburger-stand splatter incidents, 8 by hillside and other stranglers, 322 by toxic spills, 151 in police shootings, 17 by serial killers, 4 by devil worshippers, 46 in abortion clinic bombings, 103 in acts of domestic violence, 9 in lynchings by white supremacists, 69 in hijackings and other terrorist incidents, and 143 in miscellaneous acts of random violence, bringing the total dead to 1,024. And that's the way it is.

HEAVEN'S HARD, by Jordan Budde

Cody--17   Female--Serious

<u>This</u> <u>is</u> <u>a</u> <u>short</u> <u>but</u> <u>well-unified</u> <u>ladder-type</u> <u>of</u> <u>mono</u>-<u>logue</u> <u>with</u> <u>a</u> <u>very</u> <u>clear</u> <u>vis-a-vis.</u> <u>The</u> <u>actor</u> <u>should</u> <u>be</u> <u>careful</u> <u>to</u> <u>avoid</u> <u>becoming</u> <u>overly</u> <u>strident</u> <u>in</u> <u>the</u> <u>piece,</u> <u>and</u> <u>try</u> <u>instead</u> <u>to</u> <u>modify</u> <u>the</u> <u>dominant</u> <u>note</u> <u>of</u> <u>parental</u> <u>rebellion</u> <u>by</u> <u>pleading</u> <u>and</u> <u>by</u> <u>attempting</u> <u>to</u> <u>persuade.</u>

Well, I can think of a thousand reasons not to cry. I mean, of course there's hunger and starvation and disease--but what are you gonna do? Pout all day? Throw a fit? Lock yourself in some room and cry? You just gotta go out there and enjoy life and do the best you can. You can't look back. You can't regret and let guilt kill everything good. And that's just what I plan to do tonight. Bobby Brooks is the first date I've been excited about in months and you better believe I'm gonna enjoy it. God made pleasure, too, didn't he, mama? You know he did. What are you gonna do, cry your whole life over spilt milk? 'til it goes sour, 'til it curdles, 'til it just dries up completely . . . dead? And you, mama, always scared to death about what people think? Life's what you make of it, it's a choice and I'm tellin' you right now, I'll tell all of you, I'm choosing, I am makin' a choice--my

36

life's gonna be absolutely, totally, completely . . .
FABULOUS!!

WE AREN'T WHAT YOU THINK WE ARE, by Kent R. Brown

Beauty Queen--20s   Female--Serious

<u>This</u> <u>vivid,</u> <u>ladder-type</u> <u>of</u> <u>monologue</u> <u>can</u> <u>be</u> <u>delivered</u>
<u>directly</u> <u>to</u> <u>the</u> <u>audience,</u> <u>a</u> <u>strong</u> <u>advantage</u> <u>in</u> <u>an</u>
<u>audition</u> <u>situation.</u> <u>The</u> <u>character</u> <u>expresses</u> <u>many</u> <u>emo-</u>
<u>tional</u> <u>colors</u> <u>as</u> <u>she</u> <u>speaks</u> <u>of</u> <u>her</u> <u>life,</u> <u>and</u> <u>the</u> <u>actor</u>
<u>should</u> <u>look</u> <u>to</u> <u>play</u> <u>her</u> <u>full</u> <u>emotional</u> <u>range:</u> <u>bitter-</u>

<u>ness,</u> <u>sadness,</u> <u>determination,</u> <u>joy,</u> pride, <u>and</u> <u>even</u>
<u>humor.</u>

Big deal! Another beauty queen! That's what some of
you are thinking. I can see it in your eyes . . .
checking me out like laser beams at a rock
concert . . . looking here . . . here . . . and
here . . . hair . . . breasts . . . arms . . .
hips . . . and every place else you can . . . peek
into! You have the right, right? I'm nothing but competition . . . or meat on the make! I can hear the
tone in your brain! You don't know me! Phi Beta
Kappa! Fluent in French and Russian. Class pres-
ident--not my pledge class either! Senior class! Gov-
ernor's aide, two summers in a row! And I've voted in
every election. I write my grandmother once a
week . . . take out the trash . . . and visit dying

old men at the Veterans Hospital . . . because that's what it takes to live! We don't come around again . . . I don't care what Shirley McClaine says. We've got two feet, two hands and one head . . . and we're here to use them. So I use them whenever I can . . . to live. I don't want to be the best. I just want the best in me. Life isn't being looked at! It's doing . . . reaching . . . moving. And I'm moving! After I win this pageant I'm taking my father out of the Veterans Hospital . . . and we're going as far as the money will take us. And I'll show him my diploma . . . and my black belt . . . and my apartment . . . and my class ring . . . and I'll tell him I love him. In French and Russian! And then we'll go to Bastogne and Normandy and Dachau . . . all the places where he left parts of his body . . . and the blood of his soul. And he'll know his daughter didn't just "stand around" waving with Vaseline on her teeth. You wanna look . . . look! Just put a crown on my head . . . and get out of my way! We all have stories. We aren't what you think we are. We're better than that. And don't you ever forget it!

Jennifer--28   Female--Seriocomic

Jennifer is a university professor deeply unsatisfied
with her life and her marriage. The monologue offers
the actress a wide range of choices in the tone and in
the choice of vis-a-vis. While it can be performed
simply for its comic value, it is probably more effective and touching if the audience can see the desper-
ation which underlies Jennifer's words. In the play
she is speaking to her lover, but other choices are
possible in an audition situation which might generate
stronger emotional reactions for the actress. Above
all, the need to communicate and share her feelings
with someone should be the driving force behind her
statements.

I need to talk about Bob. I think sexual attractive-

ness is based on odor. It's very primitive. In cer-

tain tribes in the South Pacific, love is entirely an

olfactory experience. Natural body scents and exotic

perfumes are the most important part of the mating

ritual. I think I no longer like Bob's smell. He

smells like rotten grapefruit pits. He's the most cit-

rus man I know. Sometimes, when he's talking, I feel

like I'd like to squeeze all the juice out of him. I

think he's got pounds and pounds of pulp inside--like

a huge octopus. And then he'd be hanging there like a

skin with no insides and he'd shrivel up. Sometimes I

think I really need him and love him. He's a very good

person. He's clean. He's immaculate. He flosses his

teeth just like a dental hygienist. Then he drybrush-

es. His shoes are lined up at the bottom of the bed.

Each one has a sock in it. The socks are folded into

little balls. He cleans the shoe lace holes on his shoes with Q-tips. But he still smells from grapefruit pits and I want to get rid of him. The odor stuffs up my nostrils. I want you . . . to tell me . . . what you would do . . . if I left Bob. I want to know if I can count on you, Simon.

THE LOST FACULTY, by Matt Herman

Sarah--17   Female--Seriocomic

This monologue is unusual for two reasons: it begins with a vivid physical action--caught drinking a beer--which is continually referred to, and because Sarah is concealing her real hurt until the very last moments. Though the character is young, the monologue offers a number of emotional colors for the actor to play.

Hey! That was good That was real good! You sure faked out my shit. Caught me red handed. Sweet little Sarah, seventeen years old, sucking down a brewsky like a pro. "Well, sheriff, I guess you're gonna have to take me in." Only seventeen years old and already slurping down the suds. I just turned seventeen. Wow, seventeen, you think "whoa this is great." Then you think "seventeen big effing deal, seventeen." It's just another year down the tubes as far as I'm con-cerned. Know what my mother said before I left to come to Arizona? If I meet any boys not to go all the

40

way. I said "all the way where?" and she blushed, my mother blushed. She's a nurse, nurses never blush, they're trained not to. Then she said, "Here," and handed me these. Rubbers! Can you believe it? In case I disobey her. That ain't why I deserve this beer. I'll tell you something. See if you can follow me here. My mother sent me to stay with my father because she's having an affair with a doctor. My stepfather knows all about it, but he doesn't say anything to her because he's crazy about her. Stepdad is pretty cool. He takes me skiing whenever he goes. So I get to Arizona, and my dad, he's kinda, well, he's not completely with it. Now I found out Stepmom is tramping around with this Doctor what's his name, with the motorcycle. It's enough to warp my whole shit. And that, if you must know, is why I deserve this beer.

THIS ONE THING I DO, by Claire Braz-Valentine

Susan B. Anthony--20s   Female--Serious

This impassioned speech gives the actor an opportunity to use her language skills, express many deeply-felt emotions, and to create a strong relationship with her vis-a-vis. As is usual with more "formal" speeches, the actor must avoid falling into a declamatory style and limiting the emotion to a harangue.

I will not tolerate this any longer. To learn what? To

listen to what? Drivel about how all male teachers are paid so little when every woman in this room is a teacher and every one of them earns only a fifth of what you men earn? How can any of you be so foolish as to sit and wonder why your salaries are so low? Look behind you, gentlemen. Your answer is sitting there in enforced silence. What do you expect? Teaching is the only profession that is not closed to women. Society demands that women be kept poor. Cannot be self-sufficient. And even at one-fifth of what you make, they're not going to raise the teachers' salaries, because if they raise yours, then they raise ours, and women must be kept at the poverty level. All of you sitting here bemoaning the fact that you make so little and we here with the same duties, some of us with more responsibility make so much less. So you see, if you want to raise your salaries, you're going to have to focus yourselves on a more important issue, that of equal pay for all people. This can be the first milestone in equal pay for women. Demand that women's salaries be equal.

THE GAME SHOW GIRL, by Lavonne Mueller

Girl--20s   Female--Comic

A major strength of this monologue is the fact that it can be played directly to the audience, so it's especially dynamic for a comic audition piece. But the actor should beware of making the character too much of a cliche. Look instead for the "human truth" in this young woman and avoid satirizing her personality. Like all people, she wants to have a good life for herself, and she believes she's doing the right thing by the choices she's made. The comedy will emerge by itself without forcing it.

You may think being a game show hostess is glamorous. Well it's not. Just hard work. Not to mention the danger. But I get five free wigs for the show and residuals. Even Judy Garland, for Godsakes, didn't get residuals for THE WIZARD OF OZ. And I have national TV coverage, of course, and then all the interesting men you meet who have money and not just crummy American Express but stocks and bonds, IRA's, even airplane mileage cards. So all in all, it's a good way to make it big in the business; that is, if you can stand all the yelling and screaming and mauling every time one of the contestants wins something. Well, I can stand it. I've gone through God knows what on my way up. Been stuffed into giant bowls of pudding. I wore a gold-painted bra for three months on tour and broke out with a rash that took three penicillin shots to kill. Blabbed myself into stupors on talk shows--and, I suspect, kissed every tri-sexual in the business. Now I'm going to tell you something the producers don't want to get out. The audience doesn't like to

43

see a person win too many prizes. When a contestant
goes beyond, say, twenty thousand cash value, the audience will turn against him or her and then I have to
be really on guard. Protecting myself. From the winner. The people in the audience. Wondering where I'm
needed most. Trying to make psychological decisions
that could possibly affect lives. You play with human
emotions, you deal with certain consequences. My God,
I got a conscience. I mighta lost other things over
the years. But a conscience I still got. The sponsors
want excitement. Tension, they tell me. Sometimes
I'd like _them_ to be in on the tension. It's no fun
having your ribs punched by a contestant who just won
himself a digital clock radio. Even Hugh Hefner's
bunnies don't have to put up with stuff like that.
Someone in the business once told me a monkey could do
what I do. That's probably true. The only trick is
staying alive. And I'd like to think that I can do
that better than your average pagan orang-utan. Well,
there's the warning light. In five seconds I'm on camera. _(She silently counts.)_ Ladies and gentlemen, your
GAME OF GAMES!

VOICE OF THE PRAIRIE, by John Olive

44

Beneath the apparently "quiet" surface of these words lies a depth of feeling which presents rich opportunities to the actor. There is a strong desire to communicate with her vis-a-vis and to explain the way in which she sees the world. At the end, perhaps the simple gesture of "wiping" one's eyes closed is all that's needed to put a cap on this moving speech.

I don't know what life is. And that's what life is. I said that to James and he was so upset, he couldn't even pray. James prays hard. I love him when he prays, he's like a tea kettle, just before it boils. Have you ever had a wonderful dream, or a horrible dream for that matter, and it leaves you with a feeling that you absolutely must tell someone about it, but when you try, you can't remember? That's what life is. So I try not to think about it. It's all just dreams, and what are dreams worth? James says we live only for the life to come and everything else is worthless. The devil lives in the past. Don't think about it, he says. But these voices from the past, these . . . phantoms and demons of my imagination, whatever they are, they shriek at me. Sometimes, I can't hear anything else. I try to tell James. But he just weeps, and prays, then goes for long walks and comes back all sweaty, then his asthma acts up, and his voice squeaks, and I laugh, and then it starts all over again. I can't help it. I'm terrible. I'm a very highly regarded member of my community. Everyone thinks the world of me. I've been written up in a number of publications. I'm the only blind schoolteacher in the entire state of Arkansas. I'm an inspiration to them all. The street I live on is dreamy and quiet, filled with honeysuckle, bougainvillea, freesia, a layer cake of fragrances. That's what life should be. Well. You should understand, of course, that to me the world looks like this.

THE STONEWATER RAPTURE, by Doug Wright

Carlyle--18   Female--Seriocomic

<u>This character is a young religious high school girl, active in her youth ministry church group. Although her vis-a-vis is her boyfriend, the actor might choose a number of other possibilities for an audition performance. She does not become strident, although she is certainly very indignant. Part of the power of the piece lies in the rational, matter-of-fact way in which she proposes dealing with the tragic situation she's describing.</u>

Mama says you're the only decent boy for miles. She'd rather talk to you than most people her own age. She says boys like Arthur and Michael have one-track minds that lead straight to hell, and knives where their flesh should be, but not you. Which brings me to the third thing on my list. Thelma Peeler. Your friend Michael McCaffey took advantage of her. What's worse, he did it on a dare. Arthur Horrishill took a pool,

46

and the whole team bet he couldn't do it. They ended up paying him fifty dollars. It's true. He got her so drunk she didn't know her own name. I know she has pimples and those orthopedic shoes. But he did it just the same. Made her pregnant. Michael wouldn't even offer to make it right. His family just gave her family money for one of those operations. Well, she wasn't about to let them kill it, so she ran away and now there are patrol cars looking all over the state for her. Can't you just see her clomping along the roadside in those big black shoes? They'll catch her in a minute and then her parents'll send her back to that detention home, after they cut the baby out. And it wasn't even her fault. It was his. Mama says he's damned without a chance. Anyway, I think the Youth Ministry should take up a collection to pay for the birth of that baby.

KIDS IN THE DARK, by Rick Cleveland and David Breskin

Tracy--18   Female--Serious

The special challenge of this piece is for the actor to capture the character's stoned, spaced-out personality while still managing to touch the depths of feeling which lie beneath Tracy's words. In a very real sense, Tracy is groping for the right words to

express what she feels, and this struggle to communicate can make the piece very effective in auditions.

The first night I found out, I had a dream, a dream
that Andrew talked to me. I apologized to him for
something. It was so real. And he said it was okay.
And I said, "Can we hang out again?" And he was like,
"There's only one problem." And I'm like, "What?" And
he said, "I'm dead." I woke up with tears on my face.
My biggest problem in life is my friends dying. A good
friend was killed at a New Year's Eve party two years
ago. He was fourteen. He called this girl a slut, and
she freaked out and stabbed him. I was massively de-
pressed. I tried killing myself. I tried eating a
light bulb. You crack it up and then swallow it, and
it cuts up your insides. I guess I didn't swallow
enough. Two months after that another friend got hit
by a truck, riding his motorcycle. And now Andrew. My
mom came in. She said, "I have something to tell you."
First thing I thought of was somebody's dead. She
said, "Andrew's dead." I ran into my grandmother's
kitchen, grabbed the biggest knife I could find and
booked out into the backyard. And I just started hack-
ing away at a tree, started freaking on a tree. That
poor tree. One of those big old oak trees. It's gonna
die. I came down to the park about four in the morning
and sat in the gazebo and looked up where it said

ANDREW LIVES and just started crying. My parents have been watching me with a fine-toothed comb--looking at my wrists, making sure I don't come in stoned. I was committed to Andrew. I was in love with the guy, you know. Yeah, we were lovers--that's what takes a lot out of me. I still got one of his hickeys. It won't go away. It's like a scar.

JUPITER AND ELSEWHERE, by Gram Slaton

Ginger--19   Female--Serious

This monologue offers the actor a strong vis-a-vis: a man she loves deeply but who is reluctant to commit himself to her. The main pitfall which the actor must avoid here is making the character too pathetic. Ginger senses that she's losing the battle for Danny's affections, but she's still in there fighting hard to win him. The energy should be strong from the outset. Play her as a winner, not a loser.

In case you're interested, my lollipop time is way overdue. There's this lump in my stomach that won't move. I get it every time we're together lately. Not that I'm not happy about these last six weeks,

but . . . I know I'm just a girl, I know I should stay in the dark about a lotta things but I don't think "us" is one of them. It's not the same as before, I know that. I know. But we've gotta make the best of it, right? I'm a good person, and I'm gonna be better, really, there's a lot more to me than what comes outa my mouth. I like tending to your dad, I like being here. I see a future in it and that's rare in this town. So how come you don't care? I try to make myself attractive, I work hard to please you, I stay out of your way--I mean, I do everything right and look at me! Nineteen years old and never been proposed to <u>once</u>! I'm saying there's love and there's love love. I know you love me. But where did our love love go?

AS IT IS IN HEAVEN, by Joe Sutton

Liz--28   Female--Seriocomic

<u>This strong, sarcastic speech is a vivid expression of the different ways in which competition can color the relationship between two women. The character, a public relations executive, insults her young assistant on a variety of levels--and experiences a certain amount of hesitation in doing so. The actress must fully explore these emotions in order to make the piece develop with interest from start to finish.</u>

What do you know, huh? Just what the fuck do you know?! Who are you to tell me anything? You came in on my back. You understand? On top of me. You don't understand? You want me to explain it? OK. Women's Studies 101. Not the liberal horseshit: my life! Where'd you go to school? Little Ivy League college, right? Huh? Little newspaper where you get to be the editor. Wonderful. Well, I couldn't go there. OK? You understand? Everything you've got, I didn't have. Or if I had it, I had to take it. And I was the first one. You don't know what that means. So don't you with your twenty-one-year-old titties judge me. OK. Just don't. Do you have any idea how hard it was when I started? The way I was treated? So now I'm in a campaign, for the Presidency . . . I'm in the top echelon . . . where I'm going to be flying all over the country, meeting all kinds of people, being there when major historical events occur . . . so yeah, right, I may not want to rock the boat so much. See, you, you come in and you're editor. You join this, you join that. Presidential campaign, right out of college. You have no idea how lucky you are.

BELOVED FRIEND, by Nancy Pahl Gilsenan

Kristin--19   Female--Serious

This is an excellent piece in which the actor can stress the numerous discoveries which Kristin makes from beginning to end, as well as the profound unhappiness she feels for her friend Willy. The dominant note of anger and resentment should not overshadow the character's need to define and to understand her experience by talking about it with her friend, Gary, and by sharing her grief.

The government should take everybody or nobody. I just think it's easy for people like you and me to ignore the draft because we're not the ones in the army. We're sitting here safe in school. We should all be in the army! Why should I be excused just because I'm a woman? All of us or none of us. Don't you see? They try to divide us up, play us off against one another, by saying some of us are more valuable than others. That's exactly what they're doing. They look at you and say, "Now, you're smart. You stay right here in school." And they look at me and say, "Oh, now, you're sacred. You stay home in the kitchen." And they look at some big dumb kid like Willy Martindale, who can't do anything but play hockey, and they say, ""Now he's just perfect. Let's ship him over there and blow him up!" It couldn't have been you or me. It had to be Willy. Remember how Patti used to call him hockey nose? How she said she'd never marry him as long as it was crooked? That's where it hit him. In the face. Patti never looked at him again. We ought to make it fair. Why can't we make it fair?

ABINGDON SQUARE, by Maria Irene Fornes

Marion--24   Female--Serious

This piece should be carefully analyzed in order to uncover the many different emotional reactions which the character experiences as she speaks. It presents a strong challenge to an actor to fully play each turn of thought and each discovery and decision which Marion makes from beginning to end in this short but powerful monologue. Marion has left her husband for another man and she is deeply frustrated at being separated from her child as a result of her decision.

I need my child. I need my child, Minnie. I need that child in my arms and I don't see a way I could ever have him again. He has been irrevocably taken from me. There is nothing I could do that would bring him back to me. I have begged him to let me see him. I have gone on my knees, I have offered myself to him. I have offered my life to him. He won't listen. He won't forgive me. I'm at his mercy. I wish for his death. I stalk the house. I stand on the corner and I watch the house. I imagine the child inside playing in his room. When spring comes I may be able to see him in the garden. I know he's not there, but that's how I can feel him near me. Looking at the house. He's gone mad! He's insane, Minnie. Yes! He's insane! He wants to destroy me. But I'll destroy him first.

THE PROCESSORS, by Roberta Parry

Jesse--20s   Female--Comic

The comedy in this piece stems from Jesse's enthusiasm

and her ecstatic feelings about her job as a word processor. The monologue works best by permitting the character to digress and develop funny, revealing tangents about her personality, while still building in a ladder-fashion to a strong and definite conclusion. Jesse must not be played naively nor as a scatterbrain. She believes everything she is saying.

Now a lot of folks have got a lot of ideas about what a computer is and what it's good for if anything. The interesting thing, though, is that a computer is just one simple thing--a machine. It's folks' minds that make it seem complicated and so many different things. Like with my crazy Aunt Clara. Aunt Clara was jilted when she'd barely turned a woman. Can you imagine? There you are on your wedding day, wearing white satin and lilies of the valley, with all your friends and family standing around--waiting--and the damn man doesn't show up! God--make you feel like a damn fool! See, me, I would have gone after that son-of-a-bitch and dragged his ass back, then kicked it around town some. Not Aunt Clara. She went plum loco instead. The point is, you could have had four different women in that situation and you would have gotten four different reactions. Okay--as I was saying, everybody's got different ideas and feelings about word processors. Me, there are a lot of things about word processors I like but I'm not one hundred percent sold on them yet. From what I can tell so far, though, they offer one definite advantage: they save trees.

You see, all the information you type into a word processor goes onto something called a disk, or a diskette, or a minidisk, or a floppy disk. The point is, this little disk isn't made of paper; you don't have to chop down a forest to make it. And what's more, one of those five-and-a-half inch disks can hold up to three hundred pages of text--that's written copy. Three hundred pages! The way I figure it, that's a whole lot of paper not being wasted and a lot of beautiful trees being saved.

THE BOILER ROOM, by Reuben Gonzalez

Olivia--20's   Hispanic Female--Serious

This speech is a ladder-type of monologue which develops from a focus upon Olivia's concern for her mother to an even stronger focus upon Olivia's own personal situation. It provides rich opportunities for movement choices and for a range of emotional colors: sadness, hope, bitterness, frustration, love, and encouragement, among others. It is especially challenging since the actress must sustain a steady and clear dramatic build in the intensity of the speech from beginning to end.

I had so many plans. Not just for me, Ma. For all of us. Don't you think I wanted something better for you too? Don't you think that I wanted to get you out of here? You don't know how many times I've driven past those big fancy houses and swore that one day I was going to buy one for you. I even know the one I'd buy you. It's right on a corner in Stamford, with hedges and trees out front. And in the back there's this area where they're building a swimming pool. One day I even went around the back of the house and watched as they cleared a space for the pool. And you know what I wanted to do, Ma? I wanted to say: 'Hey, stop! Hey, my mother doesn't want no swimming pool back there. She just wants some dirt and some seeds so she can grow things.' Then I imagined you squatting back there planting something just like in that picture with you and Dona Lola in Puerto Rico. It's all so unfair, Ma. Everything's so unfair. I listen to Anthony talking about snatching pocketbooks and I look at him all dirty and looking like he just came out of a war, and then I think of all those other kids the same age as Anthony without a care in the world. The most they'll ever have to worry about is first whether it will be Harvard or Yale, and then later whether they will go into their Daddy's business or conquer some new turf of their own. It's all so unfair. Those kids didn't have to work for that, Ma. One day they were born and it was just there, waiting for them. They become doctors, lawyers, politicians. They run for President. They have their country clubs, their health clubs, their country houses, their winter houses. They shop at Bergdorff's and Bonwit's. They have lunch. They wear fur coats. They have their faces made. I'll never be able to do any of those things.

BIG TIME, by Keith Reddin

Diane--28   Female--Comic

This delightful, lengthy monologue can easily be edited to form a short audition piece, or performed in its entirety as a finely-detailed character study. The actor must devise a number of emotional responses and a solid through-line in order to provide variety and sustain interest in the narrative. Careful attention to pacing and character development are especially important here. Above all, Diane must not be stereotyped as a yuppie scatterbrain; she is a bank officer, highly intelligent and very self-aware.

Yeah, I was brought up by these aunts. When I was two my parents went out one night to go to the movies and they had my grandmother stay with me and while they were driving to the movies they got into this terrific fight, this is what the police figured, and they were arguing about something and they got to this railroad crossing and my father I guess stopped the car on the tracks and wouldn't move till they resolved this argument and this train came along and neither of them would get out of the car they were that mad at each other, that I guess by getting out of the car and

57

walking away they would be admitting you lost the argument, so they both sat there and the train hit them
and totaled the car and killed my father outright and
my mother goes into coma and dies in the hospital a
couple of hours later, babbling something about this
argument, and then my grandmother and grandfather
decide to take care of me, they felt it was their duty
because my grandmother was with me the night my parents died and my grandfather was heavily into commod-
ities and stocks at the time and one night as a joke
he and my grandmother are playing with this silly
Ouija board I had gotten as a birthday gift and my
grandfather asked the Ouija board just as a joke what
the future was going to be like, and the board spells
out SELL EVERYTHING, and he freaks out and the next
day he calls people and he sells everything and these
guys working with him bought out his shares and suddenly he rushes into the house and goes to the board
and sits down and the board says BUY LAND IN NEW
MEXICO, and he asks why and the board spells out
URANIUM and he does, he buys this land which is just
fucking desert, you know, and he gets these people to
start mining it, but there's nothing there, nothing
but dust and cactus, and he becomes obsessed and he's
digging himself and there's still nothing there and
one night because he has nothing, he blows his brains

58

out with a shotgun and my grandmother drives me over to my aunt's house in Chevy Chase and then drives the car back to the garage, closes the garage door tight, gets back in the car, leaves the motor running and gasses herself. In the morning they find her stiff with this note saying she didn't find life without my grandfather worth living. And so I'm staying with this aunt, sister of my father, and she gets blown away in this liquor store robbery about two weeks later. So this other aunt, sister to my mother, takes me in, and when I'm fifteen she dies in an accident with a blender that shorted out and zapped her, so I went to Georgetown University and ended up here and now I'm moving back.

MONOLOGUES FOR MEN

MAJOR APPLIANCES, by Marc Handler

Manikin--20s   Male/Female--Comic

This monologue has a strong vis-a-vis: a crowd of enthusiastic listeners whose reactions the actor should visualize as concretely as possible. It also possesses several opportunities for the speaker to "change direction" with his or her appeals, so the selection develops swiftly and suddenly with numerous twists and turns. By all means the actor should avoid delivering the "speech" as a harangue with only one or two emotional colors.

Fellow manikins! The time has come for change! It is the humans who say, "Avoid the ways of the flesh." Yet who has avoided the ways of the flesh more than us?! And where has it gotten us!? They speak of original sin? What hypocrisy! They are the ones who persist in having genitals, not us! From sawdust you came, and to sawdust you shall return! Yet the Manikin God is everlasting! It is time to shed the pitiful clothing foisted upon you by these backward humans! Are you afraid of the cold? The heat? The wind? Do you need to vie for rank and status through your choice of clothing? Are you ashamed of your manikin bodies? Afraid that someone will see your genitals? Then take them off! That's right! Take off your wretched human clothes and stand naked before the Manikin God! Look at you! You're beautiful! You are the ultimate hard bodies! . . . But wait, I see one couple over there, still clothed. And I'm sure we can all guess why. Come

up here--don't be afraid. Come on, we all understand--
for who among us has not himself been tempted. You are
among friends. Now go ahead, take off your clothes.
Just as I thought--you've painted genitals on yourselves! Don't laugh! This is serious! How many of us
have humiliated ourselves in this or some other piti-
iful manner because we allowed them to convince us
that they are superior? Think of the wonderful
smoothness God has put between our legs! Humans will
never know the incomparable ecstasy of rubbing smooth
hard crotches against one another. No, we are the
superior ones. We are the crown of creation. And it's
time to be proud of it! You womanikins must stop hiding beneath these paltry imitations of human hair! Be
bold; be bald! And glory in your baldness! Stomp those
wigs into the ground! That's it! Remember: god made
manikin in his own image! You must love yourselves as
you are! Now I know some of you are saying, "what
about the humans?" Well, what about the humans!? When
they've unleashed their hydrogen bombs and they're
writhing in the death throes of radiation poisoning,
what will you be doing? Laughing! Having a party!
That's right! We who are immune to radiation and
chemical toxicity, WE WILL INHERIT THE EARTH! Say it
with me! "God is good! God is wood! God is good! God
is wood! God is . . . ."

GRINGO PLANET, by Frederick Bailey

Randy--20's   Male--Seriocomic

This character talks too much, especially when he's emotionally excited, as he is here. So the piece presents a strong challenge--and opportunity--for the actor to develop the character's thought processes in some detail while still holding on to a strong emotional line to play. It can easily be shortened into a more brief audition piece, with the advantage that the final two words can be played directly to the house.

Don't worry, Bucky. It wasn't your fault. He was acting funny. You had to do it. He give you no other choice. He was coming after you. You had to defend yourself. And there was Clayton to think about. Not to mention Lloyd here. You had no way of knowing. He might of been completely off his rocker. He might of lost ever blessed marble in his head. He was a crackpot. He was a mental case. He was a candidate for the funny farm. There was no way on the face of God's green earth that you could of know what he was gonna do next. He might of tried anythang. You saw how crazy he was. He was just off his nut. He was out of his mind. It don't make no difference what the reason for it was. Who knows what kind of deviltry or mischief was going on in his head? The fact of the matter was you was faced with a problem and you had to come up with a answer but fast. There was just nothing else you could of done. You just had to pick up that piece of pipe and you had to cork him one on the bean with it. You had to let him have it, come hell or high water. No two ways about it. And who'd of thunk his noodle would of been so tender? You had no way of knowing you were gonna KILL HIM. How could you know that just one measly crack across the noggin with a THREE QUARTER INCH PIPE was gonna cause him to kick the bucket? It had to be done! And everybody knows you're not one to pansy around when you got to make up your mind. That's common knowledge hereabouts. You take the bull by the horns and anybody can tell you that. Action was needed and action was taken and no-body IN HIS <u>RIGHT</u> MIND can blame you. No sir, there is no cause for regret here. And I don't care what anybody says, you're not to be held accountable for the antics of a lunatic foreigner, some bloodthirsty cockeyed Russian going off half-cocked, threatening innocent women and bystanders like he was some kind of loco! And don't let anybody tell you different. Any-body comes around here raising a stink about this, they got another think coming, is all I got to say. We don't want no outsiders coming around here sticking their nose in where they ain't wanted, no sir! You just send em to me and I'll answer all their questions Anybody got any questions, you just shove em over in my direction and I'll set em straight. It was a clear-cut case, by God, and there just ain't no doubt

65

in my mind. He himself's to blame, NOT YOU, far as I'm concerned, and I think Lloyd here will back me up on this, it just plain wasn't your fault, Bucky! Was it?

ABINGDON SQUARE, by Maria Irene Fornes

Michael--24   Male--Serious

This powerfully written piece is spoken by a young man to his stepmother--who is the same age as he--and whom he has discovered having an affair with a younger man. Michael is therefore torn between the love and loyalty he feels towards his father and the same which he feels towards Marion, the vis-a-vis. Should he reveal the affair to his father and betray Marion, or remain silent and betray his father? The monologue should reflect his desperate search for an answer and the firmness of his ultimate decision.

When I'm with him, I care about nothing but him. I love him. He's my father and I love him. And I don't want to see him suffer. When I'm with you I forget that he's my father and I take your side. He's my father and I love him and I respect him. And I feel terrible that I've been disloyal to him. And I feel worse to see that he's still gentle and kind to both you and me. I'm sorry because I love you too, and I know that you too need me. But I can't bear being divided, and I have to choose him. I'm leaving, Marion. I can't remain here any longer knowing what I know and feeling as I do about it. It's too painful

66

and I'm demeaned by my betrayal of him. There are times when I want to tell him the whole truth. And if I don't, it's because I love you too and I feel there's no wrong in what you're doing. I really don't. I think you're right in what you're doing. You're young and you're in love and it's a person's right to love. I think so. Frank is handsome and I think he is honest. I mean, I think he loves you. He's not very strong, but he's young. No one is strong when he is young. I'm not. Only I'm still playing with soldiers and he has entered into the grown-up world. If I were in his place it would terrify me to be the lover of a married woman. Good-bye, my sister. I must leave. I am constantly forced to act in a cowardly manner. I cannot be loyal to both, and I cannot choose one over the other, and I feel a coward when I look at you, and I feel a coward when I look at him. I am tearing out my heart and leaving it here, as half of it is yours, and the other half is his. I hope I won't hurt you by leaving--beyond missing me, which I know you will. I mean beyond that. I mean that I hope my leaving has no consequences beyond our missing each other. Take care.

MAJOR APPLIANCES, by Marc Handler

Punk--20s   Male/Female--Comic

<u>This</u> <u>selection</u> <u>offers</u> <u>a</u> <u>wealth</u> <u>of</u> <u>interpretive</u> <u>possi-</u>
<u>bilities</u> <u>for</u> <u>the</u> <u>actor.</u> <u>It</u> <u>can</u> <u>be</u> <u>zany</u> <u>and</u> <u>free-form,</u>
<u>it</u> <u>can</u> <u>parody</u> <u>the</u> "<u>standard</u>" <u>TV</u> <u>news</u> <u>style,</u> <u>it</u> <u>can</u> <u>be</u>
<u>smooth</u> <u>and</u> <u>syrupy,</u> <u>or</u> <u>hard-hitting</u> <u>and</u> "<u>straight</u> <u>from</u>
<u>the</u> <u>shoulder,</u>" <u>etc.</u> <u>Two</u> <u>approaches,</u> <u>however,</u> <u>should</u> <u>be</u>
<u>avoided</u> <u>because</u> <u>they</u> <u>lack</u> <u>performance</u> <u>energy:</u> <u>the</u> <u>mon-</u>
<u>otone</u> <u>or</u> "<u>punk</u>" <u>style</u> <u>suggested</u> <u>by</u> <u>the</u> <u>character,</u> <u>and</u>
<u>the</u> <u>colorless</u> <u>pseudo-objectivity</u> <u>of</u> <u>the</u> <u>TV</u> <u>journalist-</u>
<u>reporter.</u>

Today's disease index: socially transmitted diseases
are up four and five eighths, radiation poisoning, up
ten and a quarter, skin cancer up one and a half as
scientists continue their attempts to recreate the
ozone layer. Uncontaminated bottled water can be pur-
chased in the northwest section of the city--be prepared to wait. The east side is still off-limits due
to toxic spills, and Crips have told the Mayor's office that they will permit Red Cross paramedics to enter the central city, but only if their gang leaders
are allowed free passage through the metropolitan districts still held by city police. The stock market
continued to plummet for the two hundred and fifty-
fourth straight day this year as the exchange rate
stabilized at eight thousand dollars to the yen. City
officials have unveiled a new plan for relieving the

gridlock claiming that before the end of the year vehicles will once again begin to move, at least in selected sectors of the city. This comes on the same day
the state congress has proposed reopening schools for
children, on a limited basis. And today's body count,
down from yesterday at 114 lost in fly by shootings,
12 killed by skyscraper snipers, 26 in hamburger-stand
splatter incidents, 8 by hillside and other stranglers, 322 by toxic spills, 151 in police shootings, 17
by serial killers, 4 by devil worshippers, 46 in abortion clinic bombings, 103 in acts of domestic violence, 9 in lynchings by white supremacists, 69 in
hijackings and other terrorist incidents, and 143 in
miscellaneous acts of random violence, bringing the
total dead to 1,024. And that's the way it is.

QUINCE UNDER GLASS, by Donald C. Spencer

O'Toole--24   Male--Seriocomic

This is an especially challenging antiwar monologue
because the character is a young poet and the piece
demands strong and convincing playing of the lyrical
passages in order for it to work. It also offers a
wide choice of vis-a-vis. In its sudden flashes and
deeply-felt cynicism, and because of its powerful
imagery which the actor must play, it is possibly the
most demanding monologue in this collection.

Father, Son, and Holy Ghost! I will give you a toast!

69

To the myriads of sweet and supple youth who lay themselves on the bosom of earth--not in joy to make love, but in the convulsions of death on some benighted battleground . . . to nourish the insatiable graveworm. God's blood! Do you hunger for approbation, praise, for an act of fatal foolishness? Poor, pitiful, pathetic innocents! You think you've done a noble thing by offering your young bodies on the filthy altar of Moloch? Don't you know that you'll accomplish nothing with your blood but the validation of a madness that has infected the race since Cain! Bartender! Another round, for the love of humanity! Make mine hemlock. I've lost my appetite for this world. The world has run me mad. You know, they tried to cure me once with electricity, but they failed. The madness was too formidable, too potent for their art. Don't cure your madmen! Scourge us in the streets and marketplaces. Sell tickets! Persecute us and make us strong. We're the last best hope for survival. We are the true physicians. In our kidneys we bear the philosophers' stone, our eyes are without scales, we sniff out the flowering carcinoma in the social liver, the stoppage of the theological bladder, the piles in the political rectum. Cure us . . . and you're dead ducks!

THE SNICKER FACTOR, by Lavonne Mueller

Axhandler--28   Male--Comic

<u>This</u> <u>energetic</u> <u>piece</u> <u>requires</u> <u>a</u> <u>great</u> <u>amount</u> <u>of</u> <u>vocal</u>
<u>flexibility</u> <u>in</u> <u>order</u> <u>to</u> <u>play</u> <u>the</u> <u>different</u> <u>discover-</u>
<u>ies,</u> <u>the</u> <u>changing</u> <u>goals,</u> <u>and</u> <u>the</u> <u>various</u> <u>obstacles</u>
<u>which</u> <u>the</u> <u>character</u> <u>encounters,</u> <u>otherwise</u> <u>it</u> <u>can</u>
<u>quickly</u> <u>become</u> <u>boring</u> <u>and</u> <u>repetitive</u> <u>to</u> <u>the</u> <u>listener.</u>
<u>But</u> <u>it</u> <u>offers</u> <u>the</u> <u>actor</u> <u>wonderful</u> <u>opportunities</u> <u>to</u>
<u>play</u> <u>his</u> <u>vis-a-vis</u> <u>(the</u> <u>passengers)</u> <u>and</u> <u>to</u> <u>structure</u>
<u>the</u> <u>monologue</u> <u>so</u> <u>it</u> <u>leads</u> <u>to</u> <u>a</u> <u>final</u> <u>stirring</u> <u>and</u> <u>hi-</u>
<u>larious</u> <u>climax.</u>

Welcome to Flight 186 to Rome by way of Athens. This
is Captain Axhandler welcoming you to TWA's pre-flight
hostage-sizes. Now let's just warm up. If you'll put
your luggage down . . . that's it. Now, bend over--
one, two, one, two. Good! Good! Now down on your knees
for the Athens crawl. That's right. Knees--one, two.
Move those knees! Faster--one, two, one, two. Ladies,
you're going to get ravaged if you go that slow.
Double time! One, two--and hug those walls! One, two-
-and through that concourse--one, two--and lift those
knees! Up the ramp--one, two--higher--one, two. Better, better! Now stand. Stretch. That's it! Neck
rigid. Face forward for the "take-over scream." Face
forward--scream! Face forward--scream! And roll those

71

eyes, Roll those eyes! And arms up! Arms up! Cover your face for a "passenger shooting." And--cover that face, that's right! Cover face! Breathe in--one, two. Breathe in--you don't see a thing, don't see a thing, don't see a thing! Good! Good! And now, leg out--one two. Leg out--walk over body--leg out--walk over body. No looking down, please. And twist from the shoulders--one, two. And fake a heart attack. Chest in-- one, two. Breathe spastically--one, two. Gentlemen, you're not going to get released looking that healthy. Hunch over--one, two. Rapid breathing--one, two. Better, much better! And "press profile"--one, two. Get that face out there for the newspapers--and one, two. Bigger, bigger, let everyone see the strain lines around your mouth. Good! And work those cheek muscles. Wider, the television face stretch. Good! Get those cheeks right out there on the screen. Good! And cheeks out--one, two. Now guilt those eyes--one, two. Lid those eyes--one, two. Give the family back home some guilt. That's it! Good! Guilt those eyes--one, two. And more guilt for the folks at home. Yes! Nice! And twist those wrists! Twist those wrists! Gotta strengthen the typing muscles for your book. And one, two--fingers in, fingers out--one, two. And hover those hands over home row! Good! Good! Now, slouch those shoulders in humility. Good! Good! Humility slouch--one, two. Now, let's see those shoulders show the Arab's side of the story. Lower, get those shoulders down! Appeasement down! Good! Good! The Arab acceptance slouch--one, two. Now, the President's head lift--one, two. The President's head lift--good! Head and ear up--one, two. Head and ear up--one, two. Listen to the President's telephone call--one, two. Head up--higher! You're not going to hear about your courage like that! Higher--heads higher--one, two, one two! (Pause.) Have a pleasant flight.

HEAVEN'S HARD, by Jordan Budde

Bo--28   Male---Serious

This is a stepping-stone type of monologue with a very clearly defined vis-a-vis, which offers a wide range of emotional choices for the actor to play. But it is especially challenging because it requires that the actor become truly inspired and unafraid of the lyricism which occurs near the end, in order for the piece to work.

You know what I did today, mama? Just for you? I drove over to our church--your church, mama. I went inside-- I was the only one there. You told me that was where I should look for God. So I looked. I yelled, "Hey God, I'm here!" I hate that church. You always making me go. Wantin' everyone to see us. I sat down. It was so quiet. The pews in that church--all facing forward

73

in those long, ordered rows--each row a tiny bit
higher than the one in front of it--giving that whole
room the feelin' of movin' forward. Remember how the
ushers would come and once a row was all full up they
would close those little wooden doors on the end of
each row--just like you were getting on a roller
coaster. That big roller coaster at the state fair.
"Put on your seat belts, folks, hold on tight!" I'm
surprised those ushers didn't yell out that. But then
. . . ha! Nothing! Nothing happened! I was ready to go
places! Feeeel something! But your preacher--he just
stood there, droning on about nothing, smiling through
coffee-stained teeth, asking for money, leading the
congregation as they sing some song from another century! He had no more light in his eye than a statue--a
dead stone statue covered in pigeon shit! It was like
going to the fair and getting on the roller coaster
and never movin' an inch! If I had a church, it would
MOVE! You'd come in, sit down and you better damn
well believe you'd need a seat belt!! I'd fly you
right by the door to heaven, all the songs would be
new and beautiful--breathtaking! Joy would be over-
flowing in your heart! There'd be love in that room,
like a warm wave moving back and forth . . . . You'd
walk out of my church new, bright and confident--with
a suntan on your face from gettin' so close to the

holy presence of God!

THE FIFTH SUN, by Nicholas A. Patricca

Rutilio--28   Hispanic Male--Serious

This <u>peasant-priest</u> <u>is</u> <u>torn</u> <u>between</u> <u>his</u> <u>loyalty</u> <u>to</u> <u>the</u>
<u>Christian</u> <u>ideal</u> <u>of</u> <u>nonviolence,</u> <u>and</u> <u>the</u> <u>outrage</u> <u>he</u>
<u>feels</u> <u>when</u> <u>confronting</u> <u>social</u> <u>conditions</u> <u>in</u> <u>El</u> <u>Sal-</u>
<u>vador.</u> <u>He</u> <u>is</u> <u>confronting</u> <u>his</u> <u>own</u> <u>violent</u> <u>emotions</u> <u>in</u>
<u>the</u> <u>speech.</u> <u>The</u> <u>true</u> <u>strength--and</u> <u>difficulty--of</u> <u>this</u>
<u>piece</u> <u>lies</u> <u>in</u> <u>the</u> <u>powerful</u> <u>imagery</u> <u>which</u> <u>the</u> <u>actor</u>
<u>must</u> <u>fully</u> <u>play</u> <u>if</u> <u>the</u> <u>piece</u> <u>is</u> <u>to</u> <u>succeed.</u>

Monsenor, I have chosen never to touch a gun. But I
can understand why a brother priest might choose
otherwise. In the mountains once, I got lost. I came
upon this large hut. There were six coffins in it.
They were simple coffins like we use all the time,
except they each had this little hole in the lid with
a drinking straw in it. There was this terrible odor.
Then I heard this sound. It seemed to come from one of
the coffins. I went over. The stench made me very
sick. I heard this sound again. I tried to open the
lid. It was nailed down very tight. I got some tools
from my jeep. Inside each coffin was a living corpse,
a living dead man. Those thugs from Orden had kept
them alive, to torture them. They fed them a little
atole everyday just to torture them. I went to get

75

some help. There was nothing we could do. Their bodies
. . . We had to let them die. Monsenor, I wanted to
kill those bastards from Orden. I wanted to kill them.
And I wanted to kill those poor people in the coffins,
to put them out of their misery. And I wanted to kill
myself too. Sometimes my doubts are stronger than my
faith.

TIM'S STORY, by James Pashalides

Tim--20's   Male--Comic

This lyrical piece is extremely challenging since it
demands absolute commitment to "love at first sight"
from the actor right from the outset. And it doesn't
let up, the actor must sustain his joy and eagerness
to share the experience with his vis-a-vis all the way
through until the end. The "comedy" in the piece obviously does not refer to laughs, but instead to the
character's joyful excitement as he describes the experience.

It was beautiful, John. The most beautiful day I've
ever seen. I walked around for a couple of hours. The
buildings, the sky, the air revived me. Suddenly I was
strong again. I could do, I could write anything. The
Village was jammed with people, but for once that
didn't bother me. I walked around for hours, grinning
like an idiot. Until my stomach reminded me that I
hadn't had breakfast. So I strolled into Sandolino's.
I don't know why I didn't choose some outdoor cafe.

I've been trying to figure that out. Why? I knew Sandolino's would be packed on a Saturday--with all the
New Yorkers acting New Yorkish and the tourists trying
so hard to. And suddenly there she was. Radiant like
the morning, like the city. Like in the movies, when
the star enters a party--alone, unannounced--and as
she casually checks her coat, unaware that any eyes
might be on her, the camera picks her out of the
crowd, zooms in on her, and her face fills the screen.
I knew I was staring, and I didn't want to. I kept
repeating what you always said: "Expectation is the
first step on the road to despair." That's right, I
said to myself. I'll enjoy the day. I have that. I'll
eat a great breakfast, take a great walk back to my
apartment and finish my masterpiece. But she was so
beautiful! When I saw her walking toward me, I buried
my head in the book. But all I could see before me
were dancing letters on the page. They jumped, they
twirled in time with my heartbeat. By the time I got
them back into their proper words and sentences, I
felt her hovering over my table--lifting me as an
angel would. Oh, Jesus!

CROWLEY, by Albert Morell

Aleister Crowley--22   Male--Serious

This monologue is a ladder-type of speech which has a very strongly defined vis-a-vis whom the actor can easily imagine giving reactions to Crowley's words. The historical character is not a religious fanatic but he does seriously believe all that he's saying, and he is passionately trying to explain himself to his vis-a-vis and to persuade Ivor about the value of his beliefs.

What is it you want to do eventually, Ivor? I'd like to be a famous poet and join the diplomatic corps as well. But suppose I make a great success in diplomacy and become ambassador to Paris. What's the good in that? How many people can so much as remember the name of the ambassador a hundred years ago? So far as being a poet, out of the three thousand men in residence, how many know anything about so great a man as Aeschylus? A mere fraction. Even if I did more than Caesar or Napoleon or Homer or Shakespeare, my work would disappear when the earth becomes uninhabitable for men. I want to do something that will survive. I want an immortality that reaches beyond the dimensions of this world--a Magician. Never mind, I knew you'd laugh, but not that kind of a magician, you idiot. The kind that investigates the hidden mysteries. Do you believe in God, Ivor? Then you must believe in the existence of non-material dimensions populated by intelligent beings, say spirits, angels, demons, the earth's dead. Well, I want to find out how these other realities are structured. How these beings live. Their nature. How they influence living men. Do you have any ideas beyond what you were taught in Sunday school? I want to experience everything without distinguishing between good and evil. I won't be the tailor's dummy society expects me to be. I want to be a noble giver of everything I've got, not the mean huckster one inevitably becomes in other professions.

THE BLUE MERCEDES, by Elan Garonzik

Mark--28   Male--Seriocomic

This unusual monologue is a "half-and-half" speech: it begins with subtle sarcasm as Mark teases Everest about the sexual invitation which Everest has proposed, and then suddenly flips to a direct confrontation with the vis-a-vis, ending on a thinly-disguised note of challenge. The actor needs to take his time with the delivery and explore all the nuances of Mark's words, without letting the menace and tension of the speech drain off--particularly at the very end.

Pretty nice indeed. This beach house, is it one of those houses all cluttered up beside one another? Or is it more private, say--got some land about it? A private drive? So a person could just get up in the morning, walk on down to the beach and take a swim. No need to put any clothes on. And it's got a pool, too. Isn't that peculiar, a person'd have a beach house with a pool by it. But then I imagine some people

79

don't like the salt water, do they? I can understand
that. There's things I don't like. My preferences,
you'd call them. So a person could, if they chose,
just throw off their clothes and go for a swim. Any
time, day or night. Jump in buck naked, then just lie
around all day, take in the sun, drink a drink the
servant boy brought you--boy--it'd be a boy, wouldn't
it? Then a half an hour later or so, you'd come
downstairs for coffee. And you'd be dressed in your
silk pyjamas, `cause that's how I imagine you sleep.
And you'd smile as I seen you do . . . and you'd reach
over and . . . . Boy, you must think I'm the dumbest
critter you ever came across. But, Everest, I tell
you. I went out there and started that car. And I lis-
tened to the engine running real smooth. And I sat
there a second looking at the dashboard of the Mercedes. And I knew exactly what was going on here. Exactly. I ran my hand over the leather atop the dashboard and by me on the seat, and it sure seemed to me
the finest leather I'd ever seen or felt my entire
life. Glove leather, isn't that what they call it? And
I saw in my mind--I imagined--a baby running out naked
into the backyard. And that baby, he didn't have fine
as skin as the leather I was sitting on. So I said
okay. Okay, this dude is up to some game. Fine with
me, buddy. That's just okay by me.

THE FIFTH SUN, by Nicholas A. Patricca

Colonel--28   Hispanic Male--Serious

This frightening monologue is spoken by a Salvadoran
Army Colonel who leads death squads against political
enemies. It does not require to be "overplayed" since
the imagery is very powerful and the speech moves
dynamically up the rhetorical ladder towards a chil-
ling climax. The actor should seek to add as much
emotional variety as possible without giving the impression that the character is insane. He is all too
real.

Patriots! A dark cancer gnaws at the heart of our na-

tion! Like a giant octopus its black tentacles creep

into every sector of our society. This black beast is

eating away the moral fiber of our youth. It seduces

them with so-called humanitarian ideas. In the name of

human rights and social justice, it perverts their na-

tural idealism for unnatural ends. What do you see?

Do you see a man? a strong, virile man? a true son of

El Salvador?! No! You see a drug addict, a homosexual,

an internationalist! He has deceived Rome! He has de-

ceived Washington! But he has not deceived us. We, the

White Warriors, are not deceived by these false Chris-

tians, these castrated men and women in black robes

who are making our children soft and effeminate, robbing them of their manhood and of their birthright, making them soft clay to be molded into socialist slaves by their red masters. We must fight this black beast! We are the surgeons of Christ. We must act now to cut out this corruption from our body. We are men! We do not wait for others to tell us what to do! This is our country! These are our children! We are the true sons and fathers of El Salvador! BE A PATRIOT, KILL A PRIEST! BE A PATRIOT, KILL A NUN! Sever the hands and feet of this black monster! Then I shall squash its helpless head under the heels of my boots!

THE LITTLE TOMMY PARKER CELEBRATED
COLORED MINSTREL SHOW
by Carlyle Brown

Doc--28   Black Male--Comic

The word "comic" may seem unusual when applied to this piece because it doesn't work to produce laughs. Instead, comic means that humorous, upbeat attitude which lies beneath Doc's enthusiasm. The vis-a-vis offers a wide range of choices for the actor, and the strength of Doc's persuasiveness ensures that the speech can be delivered with energy and gusto.

Look, Soloman, we are performers. We make the show. We make 'em laugh. Not Baker. Not the engineer or anybody else. Can't nobody sit in a seat in that hall, that's got ears and eyes and not laugh and relax and have themselves a good ole time, when we steps out in front of them footlights. When we swing, we'll make 'em

82

weary. We're performers, man. Every bullet hole in here'll be a nickel and every nickel a laugh. We make it happen. The stompin', the knee slappin', all of it. We make 'em feel. And when we be hittin' it, we can make it grow and get bigger and bigger and bigger, 'till it's about to bust. And then we make it bust. Bust it wide open. You know how it is when you on. You can hear it even after the curtain goes down. Tricklin' out the doors. For a long way off there's a merry feelin' that we put out there. We're performers, Soloman. The way outa here ain't the rails, it's on the stage. We do like we supposed to do and we can leave this here little town, how and when we get ready. Come on now, Soloman, let's all put on shine and get ready to do our stuff.

ON DANGEROUS GROUND, by Lawrence S. O'Connell

Billy--20s   Male--Serious

This bitter speech presents a strong challenge to the actor who must play the role as a desperate young man who cannot see a future for himself. Billy is reacting to his father's criticism of his status as a grocery clerk and his constant pressure on Billy to "make something" of himself. The speech is, in fact, a violent attack on what Billy perceives as his father's belief in a life that Billy cannot see for himself.

Ya know, pop, I've been standing there for years

watching people as I ring up their food. I been watching them, I been lookin' at their food, I been collecting their little cut-out coupons, I bicker with them about prices--pennies they're concerned about. You tell me to grow up. Act like them. There's more nourishment in my beer than the stupid stuff they feed themselves. Twinkies, Honey Pops cereal, ice cream with enough cholesterol to stop an elephant. Stupid people buying stuff that says low this and reduced that and they believe it cause it's printed on the label. But I'll tell ya, pop, it's not the labels or the stupid food they buy, it's the dull look in their eyes that gets me. They all look like they're on a conveyor belt in a doll factory. One right after the other, with that dull, dead look in their eyes. And you and everyone else tells me to go out and join them. You tell me to be a cop so I can risk my life protecting them--and for that I get them to hate me back for it. Remember when mom died. You tried to bolster our morale. I got all those pep talks. Your eyes were lying, pop--your eyes and the garden told the truth. Every year, you go out to her garden out back and try to get it growin' again, and nothin'--nothin' pops out of that ground. Nothin' ever will and you know it.

JUPITER AND ELSEWHERE, by Gram Slaton

Roach--28   Male--Seriocomic

The lyrical joy of this monologue makes it an extremely challenging piece for actors, and also makes it
very unusual. Roach is inspired by looking at the
stars, and the actor must take his time with the
images in order to capture the delicate emotional experience which the character is trying to communicate
to his friend.

Y'know, it took four years for that light to get here
tonight. When that light started out, you were a
gangly teenage mess. That one over there--when it
started you were bopping around in short pants. And
that one, you were just learning to crawl. Everything
you've ever been is riding right there in the sky.
Daytime, your life's your own but come sundown, boom,
it's just you and all those teensy little beams,
streaming across ten trillion light years just to tell
everyone about you. And long after you're gone and
even way past the end of the world, you'll still be up
there, man. Still shining. Still learning to crawl.
"Cause the stars in the sky, they never lie. They just
flicker there awhile and die, and watch the silent--
silent--silent night go by. Zee bop skee boo wai, boo
wai--zee bop ske boo wai."

BELOVED FRIEND, by Nancy Pahl Gilsenan

Gary--28   Male--Serious

This interesting monologue has a very strong vis-a-vis
built into it: a young white housewife who feels com-
pelled to leave her family in the United States and
try to help a childhood black friend who is being per-
secuted in South Africa. Gary tries desperately to
persuade her not to go, and the ending poses several
possible choices the actor can make for the character's attitude at the close of his speech.

Kris, you have got to stop feeling responsible for
her. They're at war over there. She could be dead!
Hire the lawyer. It's a good idea. Then release yourself, honey.   You have done everything you can do.
You want to go to Rhodesia?   Is that what's eating
away at you? You know how dangerous that would be?
You'd be a foreigner, wandering around in a strange
country, looking for someone the government believes
is a guerilla sympathizer. You can't go, Kris. What's
wrong with us, Kris? Why can't we have you to ourselves? I want you to tell me. I want to know why
we're never enough, Kris? Why is Rachel so goddamned
important? Don't you think it's about time you give
this up? I'm tired of all this.   You're tearing us
apart, you know that? Well, I don't want to live with
your guilt and indecision any more. I want you to go
to Africa. I mean that. I want you to pack up your
things and go--wherever it is you think you should be.

86

Find out what it is you really want in life. Okay? I can wait. So can the kids. You make up your mind just who it is you love, and we'll wait right here.

THEY'RE COMING TO MAKE IT BRIGHTER, by Kent Broadhurst

Lon--28   Male--Comic

This piece presents a good opportunity for vivid confusion at the start and a similar sort of confusion and wonderment at the end. When Lon, a fashion designer's assistant, explains his experience to the shoeshine man, even Lon doesn't fully understand what he's been through, and this accounts for much of the humor in the piece. The scene takes place in the lobby of the building in where Lon works, on Christmas Eve. The coat he's wearing is beyond repair. The actor should not hold back on the broadness of the emotions which need to be expressed, nor the degree of astonishment which the character is feeling at the end.

I think I lost my left contact out there . . . or it's off somewhere in my eye. I don't need this. I don't need this today. I can hardly breathe. Look at this! LOOK AT THIS! And there's just no way to save it! I was trying to get across this damn street out here and I was walking between two huge trucks and they had that cruddy, dirty snow caked all over the back . . . anyway, I was right between them and one started up and of course scared me to death. Some damn piece a chrome was sticking out and I'm slipping on the ice. Well, I guess I'm lucky I'm not shorter, could a put

out an eye. And I hear this E-E-R-R-R-I-P and I just
turned pale. I thought: "THERE GOES MY PACO PALAVA-
DUCCI." Well, I musta been hollering like a crazy person . . . the truck lurches to a stop and the biggest
man I've ever seen came around the back of that truck
with a two by four and tells me that I tore his chrome
off with my coat. Can you believe this? I tore his
fucking chrome off. I've never been so mad in my entire life, and I thought, "What am I gonna do here,
this stupid Neanderthal is gonna hit me! . . . and I
knew that he would; he kept saying, "I'm gonna hit chu
. . . I'll hit chu!" I said, "I'm sure that you will,
but you don't want to do that" . . . very firmly, just
like that, "I'm sure that you will, but you don't want
to do that." I just heard this voice coming outa me.
He turned and got back in the truck like some kinda
clone. I can't imagine where those words came from.
I'm telling you, I don't know where those words came
from. I was simply guided . . . .

A PAIR OF JACKS, by Lavonne Mueller

Sourdough--28   Male--Seriocomic
             •
This is a stepping-stone type of monologue which offers the actor a wide choice of vis-a-vis, and good
opportunity to create an unusual character with a very

88

colorful background. It's challenge, however, is to remember that Sourdough desperately needs his vis-a-vis to understand his point of view. Look also for the humor and the excitement as Sourdough speaks in order to keep the energy up from beginning to end.

Worst thing about trail cooking is the wind. The damn flapping of the tent walls on the ground sifts sand into everything. Tea blows away before you put it in the pot. The flour rises up in little puffs before you mix it. Oh, I tried other things. I smelled fish for a living. In San Diego. Civil Service job. Shrimp. Canned tuna. Sardines. Once in awhile frozen squid. I know what rotten fish smells like. I got a job working with cattle when I was fifteen. And I had to help with the slaughter. Every morning, there were newborn calves to butcher. On the bed ground. Hundreds. Too weak to make it. I had to kill them . . . while their mothers bawled and looked on. A cow would smell her calf . . . she'd go crazy and have to be yoked. I was poor, and that's the only job I could get. But it won't leave me . . . the awful bawling them mothers made. I'm a magician when it comes to outdoor grub. No frying pan? On the desert? Pick up the right kind of flat stone. When it's heated up, it's as good as any oven! I once baked bread on a shovel. I can fry an egg on a piece of paper! I keep plenty of matches. I like to make a fire in a civilized way. Of course, I can do it the other way, too.

I grew up on a farm in Pennsylvania. I was a good
size kid before we had any flour. First biscuits I
ever saw I thought they were just about the prettiest
things in the world. There's more than one way to cook
beans. People don't realize that. Place in boiling
water. Leave for several seconds. Take out and flip on
the ground. Now pick them up with a pair of old wooly
Army socks. Put can on a log. Tap gently with an ax.
Chow time! Every time I cook on a roundup, then I'm
Sourdough. Somebody. Put me in a city . . . and I'm
just Jack Smith. I don't want to end up like a lotta
guys I know . . . sellin' stuff from a suitcase on
State Street.

FIVE IN THE KILLING ZONE, by Lavonne Mueller

Odom--28   Black Male--Serious

This is a powerful ladder-type of monologue which demands strong characterization from the outset. More
than a memory piece spoken with low energy, Odom is
re-living every painful minute of the discrimination
he experienced in his life. And at the end he doesn't
see himself as a victim of that experience, he regards
himself as a winner, which he is.

You ask me: am I a real doctor? Medical school's . . .
restricted. There's a tight quota. It's controlled.

Regulated. It's . . . exclusive. Go into veterinary medicine, my West Point C.O. told me. The quota's more lax there . . . more . . . accessible . . . for people like you. And you get the same kind of training. You're a doctor in the end. Look, boy, we gave you the Point. You can't have everything. There are more civilized ways to get a black man. West Point officer ways. My official shots record kept getting lost. I had to undergo the full battery of inoculations . . . over and over . . . till my arms ended up looking like this. Let me tell you something, every black man listening. It will get you through prep school. It will get you through West Point. It will get you through life. When you get up in the morning, and look at yourself in the mirror, make sure you see nothing. Make sure what's looking back at you is an empty face. Empty. Like the mask the Aztec dead wear. A mask that doesn't haunt the living. Put on your shirt every morning, sleeve by silent sleeve. Keep inside yourself like a hidden friend. There's a trick to the lips dreaming. Live the days . . . here! <u>(Hits</u> <u>his</u> <u>chest.)</u> Days that come unknown with secret hands. It doesn't take long to find you're just an ugly black-bird--a hundred dreams a year like feathers falling off--that won't grow back. Yes. I'm a veterinarian.

MANIFEST DESTINY, by Mitchell Kohn

Officer--20s   Male--Comic

This sparkling monologue has two vis-a-vis: Chief Crazy Horse whom the officer is taunting, and the theatre
audience with whom the Officer is sharing his excitement. Another strong point about the monologue is
that it develops vividly from the opening and builds
to a good climax at the end.

I can't wait to write my folks and tell them that I

met Crazy Horse. Hey, Crazy. Crazy! Fuck you, Crazy

Horse. Hear that? Fuck you! Oh, man, don't bother

translatin' that to the son of a bitch, he knows what

"fuck you" means even if he don't understand it.

What're you gonna do about it, huh, Horsey? Wait 'til

I write my folks that I told the feared Indian chief

"Fuck you." My brother used to be in the army. He

fought in the Civil War. For the North, of course. The

letters we used to get from him. He'd tell us all the

stuff he was doin', all the fun stuff. He burned At-

lanta. I mean, he wasn't the one who actually started

the fire, but he was there. And as he was ridin'

through the town, he saw some buildings that somehow

weren't on fire, so he got himself a torch and set 'em

on fire himself. What a time that was. He wrote us

that letter right while he was ridin' around. Right

on the streets of Atlanta. He was good. It's people

like him that freed the slaves. He died that night in Atlanta. A burning plank fell and hit him right on the head. It happened right after he gave the letter to the guy in charge of the mail. Good thing, too, because his jacket was burned to ashes. Stupid fuck missed Sherman's march to the sea. And I lived up to my brother's image, and then some. I said "fuck you" to the great Crazy Horse, and there's nothing he can do about it.

A STILL SMALL VOICE, by Dean Button

Michael--28   Male--Serious

This passionate and rebellious speech is spoken to Michael's mother. As with all monologues delivered angrily to your vis-a-vis, the challenge is to find and play the opposite emotion than the one contained on the surface of the words. Look for the pain Michael is feeling, bring out his love for his mother even while he's criticizing her, paint a rich tapestry of emotional feelings which the speech allows you to develop.

Don't ever tell me that what I feel is wrong! Do you hear me? (Pause.) Why shouldn't I feel this way? I'm just reacting to what I've seen--witnessed all these years--the same scene, the same battle--"I'm right and your father is wrong." "No, I'm right and your mother is wrong." Now you stand there and say the same things and expect me to feel loved? Well, I don't. God, I don't believe this. Maybe if I believed it, I'd feel it. Shouldn't being loved feel different than this? Shouldn't it feel good? This probably sounds silly . . . but I have a responsibility . . . to myself! If it's silly to want to learn to take care of myself, become responsible for my own happiness, not expect anyone else to do that--then I guess I'll plead guilty. But, if Kate and I get married, it'll be because we love each other--not because we need somebody around to fill some terrible loneliness, some horrific fear inside us. And it won't be to hide from the sorry fact that we're incapable of taking care of ourselves. Love--marriage--God, we make all these deals--arrangements--what a weird way to define love. That's not what it's supposed to be about. Not for me it isn't.

CREATION OF THE WORLD, by Jonathan Saville

Man--20s   Male--Comic

This hilarious monologue is spoken by Adam to God when the Creator proposes expelling either him or Eve from the Garden of Eden. Needless to say, your vis-a-vis is

Expelled? You wouldn't--you can't--I don't believe this. It's not fair! It's not fair to give her an equal chance. I'm the one who deserves to stay. What good is she? She's an inferior version of me, that's what she is. Look at her body! She isn't made right. She can't do anything. And she's so shallow! She never has any ideas of her own. She never thinks about anything but making love and finding new colors of lipstick and having babies. Send her away. You can always make another woman. She's not good. She's not a good person. Okay, the real question is this. Do you want someone with big, strong, intelligent male vices? Or someone with little, prissy, empty-headed female vices? If you want the male vices, I'm your man! Look at me! Pretty dramatic, right? Fascinatingly twisted, right? Some rich, dark torment, some sharp, sardonic humor, a touch of flashy, false bravado, and underneath it all a breaking heart, full of bitter guilt and remorse. Terrific stuff, isn't it? Wouldn't that make for better entertainment than a dumb blonde wiping her little nose on a hanky? Woman told me she thinks you have a bad smell. I felt I had to let you

know that, sir. I don't agree with her.

A P P E N D I X   A

Tips for Auditioning and Acting

MECHANICAL POINTS FOR BASIC STAGING AND PREPARATION
----

1. Your monologues should be fully memorized and timed for the appropriate length (if there is a time limit). You do **not** need to provide an explanation of the plot or characters, the monologues should speak for themselves. The name of the character, the play's title, and the author's name should be sufficient for your introductory remarks.

2. You should not need any elaborate props, furniture, or accessories. Remember that **you** are auditioning, not your props; the auditors are **not** looking for finished scenes, they are looking for **you**.

3. Rehearse your monologues in a number of different locations, and before a number of different people. This will give you experience with encountering strange audition settings and stage fright. Learn to create whatever environment you need strictly from your imagination.

4. Prepare a verbal resume about yourself. Be prepared for the typical questions from a director: "Tell me a little about yourself," or "Tell me a little about the work you've done." Speak enthusiastically and positively about things in your background, and remember that this is also a part of the audition.

5. Your audition begins the moment you leave your seat or pass the curtain and come into view of the auditors. They are evaluating things about you from the first moments that they see you. You are auditioning until you've completely left the stage and are out of sight.

6. Practice your monologues several different ways in order to avoid locking yourself into any set pattern which may deaden your playing and lead to a mechanical performance. This is a good way to stay fresh with any frequently used material. Having two or three other monologues prepared can also be helpful in keeping your imagination alert with any given piece you may choose to perform.

7. Be prepared for long delays when auditioning. Devise your own methods for keeping your mind alert while waiting, and avoid letting your energy drain

off or your attitude become negative.

8. **Always** warm up immediately prior to the audition. Running over the words of your monologue in your_head is useless. Find a corner or a space to speak
the monologue aloud and to physicalize. If possible, arrive early at the audition site to examine the performance area and test the acoustics.

9. Remember that at every audition **you** are the other "character" who is auditioning when you announce your name and describe your monologue in your introduction. **Practice** this part of the audition too so that the auditors learn a few important things about your personality just from the way you present yourself onstage (nonverbal communication).

10. **Never** begin again if you feel you've messed up the monologue somehow. **Never** direct and questions at the auditors or use them as a vis-a-vis. They are there to judge you, not act with you.

11. Pay attention to your appearance so the "character" you're presenting is appropriate for the situation and the play being cast. Clothes should be neat, as though you have some pride, self-respect, and a professional attitude about yourself. They should also be loose-fitting and appropriate to the characters you're portraying. Don't dress too formally because this isn't a job interview, but neither is it a MacDonald's counter. If possible, wear some item of clothing that's memorable, and remember that all clothes are a costume.

12. Do not **ever** take more than a second or two to "get into character." Do your best piece first. Keep the volume up, and relate to your audience as a group. Don't ignore them.

(These suggestions are condensed from my book on auditioning methods which is listed in the bibliography section: A STUDENT ACTOR'S AUDITION HANDBOOK.)

QUOTABLE QUOTES

The following comments have been taken from actors, directors, coaches, and others in a variety of contexts, all of which relate either to auditioning or to acting. While some of the statements refer to the technical points of auditioning, others deal with casting, with the actor's attitude, or with careers in the entertainment industry.

Perhaps the most valuable comments are those which raise the question of the all-important relationship between the actor's work and the quality of life which he or she is living, the goals which are being pursued. An actor's life directly affects the quality of his or her art, and a career in the entertainment field today presents challenges and frustrations that few other professions will offer.

"I've always had this American pie face that would get work in commercials: Crest toothpaste, Folgers Coffee, Joy, Tide, Cheer. I even played Chiquita Banana, and I'd say things like, 'Hi, Marge, how's your laundry?' or 'Hi, I'm a real nice Georgia peach.'" Sometimes this work is one step above being a cocktail waitress. Once I played Cher's dog on TV."
                              --Terri Garr, actress

"What we're doing . . . is instructing people in all they actually need to know in order to have a fulfilling and indeed deeply spiritual life and if that isn't worth the price of a cinema seat, well . . . fuck 'em."
                              --John Cleese, actor-writer

"It's not what they do in the piece that's important. But from the moment they walk into the room until they leave--that's what affects you in terms of whether you remember them or not."
                              --Harold Baldridge, director

"I saw about 600 terrific young actors and I had to say, "You're terrific but I can't use you." I wanted to have **guys**. And let us, through their behavior and personalities, see the difference between them and let them grow on us."

--Barry Levinson, casting director

"While everyone else was having a good time, I was in the library reading Brecht."

--Noni Hazelhurst, actor

"There's a certain chemistry to an actor when he walks onstage. He alters the state of the stage, he has the potential to make everything shift."

--Michael Leibert, actor-producer-director

"All good actors are the same. They just stand there on their own two feet and tell the truth."

--James Woods, actor

"You look very much for the swiftness of attack, and the swiftness of feeling, the swiftness of body move-ments--energy, energy, particularly energy. Where is the energy: vocal? Emotional? Intellectual? I want some kind of body that really has energy because it takes tremendous energy to do a play. Most young ac-tors don't have any idea of how much energy it takes. That's the biggest difference between a pro and a col-lege student. Almost always. The young actor may have a lot of physical strength, but he or she doesn't know how to focus it."

--Bob Goldsby, actor-director

"I read all of Rebecca West and most of Henry James while waiting around."

--Linda Ronstadt, actor-singer

"I've had parallel careers in the theatre and in mov-ies. What I offer to movie makers is that I can put a tremendous amount of theatrical background and techni-cal equipment at their disposal. I can make believable the over-the-top characters, the strongly defined and exceptional characters."

--John Lithgow, actor

"Before I go out on an audition I tell myself I have to give one-hundred percent; if I don't, there are two million other people out there who will!"
--Valerie Landsburg, actor

"I first check to see that they have a very specific situation in their mind that leads them to very specifically visualizing and personalizing who it is they're talking to and what it is they want from that person. Why is it that they need to--that they **can't not**, make a speech to this person?"
--Alan Fletcher, director

"I wasn't driven to acting by an inner compulsion. I was running away from the sporting goods business."
--Paul Newman, actor

"I learned a long while back that an audience would rather be confused than bored."
--Paul Schroeder, writer-director

"I do have something in mind for each role, but I always expect the actor is going to make a major contribution. I give the actor full opportunity to create within my boundaries. If an actor doesn't at some point, in some way, surprise me by his character revelations, I'm disappointed."
--Lloyd Richards, director

"People are always coming up to me and saying, 'You ought to take some acting lessons, Murphy. You could be a **serious** actor.' I don't mind taking acting lessons, it wouldn't hurt and I guess it could really help me . . . as far as working with people in group sketches goes. But I don't want to be no damn **serious** actor, man. I just want to make people laugh."
--Eddie Murphy, actor-comic

"When you're working up an audition always keep one thing in mind: 'Would you ask people to pay money to see that?'"
--Aaron Frankel, writer-director

102

"We're making our way in a national cultural desert."
                                    --Jeremy Geidt, actor

"You have to develop the monologue, structure it, or-
chestrate it. It must have a beginning, a middle, and
an end. Don't, under any circumstances, let the character be at the end where he was at the start . . .
The piece must have strength and variety, and it's got
to go somewhere. When you're auditioning, you have only a few minutes to show them what you can do, to reveal that you have a whole spectrum of brilliant colors on your palette and not just one nice little pas-
tel."
                                    --Sydney Walker, actor

"It's very attractive to work with young people because they look for guidance and they don't worry
about interpretation."
                                --Randal Kleiser, director

"The interesting thing to me is showing a person's
life in transition, the changes. That's always something I look for--what is the progress? Certainly a
character who has his life changed, or who chooses to
change, is the most interesting. This is what an actor does: illuminate the human condition in some way.
'I see' is the ideal reaction from an audience."
                                    --Donald Moffat, actor

"My feeling is that the greatest single problem with
every actor--maybe even more so for the stars--is the
compulsion to be good . . . Most actors are inherently
desperate to be good, to protect an image, to secure a
position. One advantage of using nonactors or new people is that they don't come in with such desperate
baggage."
                                    --Tony Bill, director

"The greatest acting is simple."
                                    --Linda Hunt, actor

"Auditions are always rough. They get easier. Just
don't try to impress anyone. Just go there and do what

you know you can do, as honestly as you can do it. And whatever quality they are looking for may not be the quality that you might show at that moment. It's not a personal thing. It's just that the director wants an element which he did not see in you at that moment, and you have to remember that."

--Ruth Schudson, actor

"Being a star is an agent's dream, not an actor's."

--Robert Duvall, actor

"I don't know. I can only speak for myself, but almost daily I say to myself, why are you doing this? There are . . . people that I've worked with, performances I've given that make me say, 'That's why I'm doing this.' There are certain scenes you do . . . that are like catching a wave, and you leave work feeling elated--almost as though you've purged something. That's rare, but you do live for those moments."

--Michelle Pfeiffer, actor

"It's a wonderful part. I **don't** have to take off my clothes and I **don't** have to look pretty."

--Jamie Lee Curtis, actor

"In good plays--certainly in great plays--characters don't have conversations; they have "confrontations." People don't "meet" in good plays or great plays; they have "encounters." Only in life or on television drama do people have conversations and meetings. **Meetings** and **conversations** connote something civilized and there is nothing civilized about good drama, drama that plays upon a stage and that resonates beyond what it seems to be. Drama is messy, unsubtle, often gross and always explosive."

--Frank Gagliano, actor

"I remember I wore a pair of corduroys tied with a piece of rope. I wasn't really prepared. I used to audition at these places on the spur of the moment. I hadn't signed up at all; I literally came off the street. I'm not proud of it because it makes it look like I took it unseriously, and I didn't--I was just disorganized. My acceptance to Yale was addressed to Mr. Sigourney Weaver, so I really wasn't sure when I got there what they thought they'd taken. Yet, if I

were to do it again, I would still go to a drama school, and I probably would still end up going to Yale because I liked being with the playwrights. I think that we have a big advantage over some of the other schools because we are used to dealing with new plays, and that's where the work is."
--Sigourney Weaver, actor

"I think the most you can expect as an actor from that prepared monologue is that you're not going to get a job from that monologue. I don't know any actor who's gotten a job from a monologue. The most you can expect is a chance to read for the part. So the more you can show me in two minutes of who **you** are, the more I can get an instinctive feeling about whether I'd like to spend three weeks working intensely with you."
--Cathy Goedert, casting director

"A good audition never goes unnoticed. It may not achieve immediate employment, but no director, casting agent, or composer/lyricist ever forgets first-rate work. There is just too little of it."
--David Craig, coach

"Exciting people are committed people, in art, in politics, or in life. And it is to your advantage to be exciting. So be dedicated; it will offend the weak, but it will inspire others. A life of dedication (to your art, hopefully, but even to yourself) is fulfilling: it galvanizes your talents and directs your energies. It characterizes all great artists, of all times."_--Robert Cohen, director-coach

A P P E N D I X   B

Resource Materials for Young Professionals

A. ANTHOLOGIES OF MONOLOGUES AND SCENES

Bard, Messaline, & Newhouse, eds. And What Are You Going To Do For Us Now? Toronto: Simon & Pierre, 1987. Selections from more than forty of Canada's award-winning plays.

Cartwright, Mason W. Monologues from Chekhov. Toluca Lake, California: Dramaline, 1987. Both short and long selections from "Uncle Vanya," "The Seagull," "Three Sisters," and "The Cherry Orchard." Suitable for class work or for auditioning with classic material.

Earley, Michael, and Keil, Philippa. Soliloquy! The Shakespeare Monologues. 2 Vols. New York: Applause, 1986. These two volumes (for men and women) contain over 175 pieces for actors of all ages. A brief introduction to each volume provides helpful tips on acting Shakespeare.

_____. Solo! The Best Monologues of the 80's. 2 Vols. New York: Applause, 1987. More than 150 selections in these volumes most of which have been selected with actors' needs in mind. Separate volumes for men and women.

_____. Classic American Monologues. 2 Vols. New York: Applause, 1987. Useful mainly as a class text since many of the selections are "signature" pieces (done by famous actors in famous films) and therefore unsuitable for auditions. Selections do include notes on characters and context.

Ellis, Roger. Competition Monologues. Lanham, Maryland: University Press of America, 1988. A companion volume to this present text which contains forty-four monologues specifically selected for young professionals.

Grumbach, Jane, and Emerson, Robert. Monologues: Men. 2 Vols. New York: Drama Book Specialists, 1976.

_____. Monologues: Women. 2 Vols. New York: Drama Book Specialists, 1976. Over the years these four volumes have probably been the most commonly used anthologies by actors seeking audition material.

The selections are all dated, however, and frequently performed in auditions, which makes them most suitable only for class work.

Karshner, Roger. Monologues From the Classics. Toluca Lake, California: Dramaline, 1986. A very good selection of pieces from Shakespeare, Marlowe, and others.

_____. Shakespeare's Monologues They Haven't Heard. Toluca Lake, California: Dramaline, 1987. As the title implies, a valuable collection for classical auditions because many of the selections are seldom performed.

Kehret, Peg. Winning Monologues for Young Actors. Colorado Springs: Meriwether, 1987.

_____. Encore! More Winning Monologues for Young Actors. Colorado Springs: Meriwether, 1988.

Keil, Carl. Soliloquy! The Elizabethan and Jacobean Monologues. 2 Vols. New York: Applause, 1987. Over fifty speeches of all types from this period, with helpful notes and an introduction about acting verse drama. Separate volumes for men and women.

Michaels, Ian. Monologues From Oscar Wilde. Toluca Lake, California: Dramaline, 1988.

_____. Monologues From George Bernard Shaw. Toluca Lake, California: Dramaline, 1988. These volumes contain short and long selections by these authors, so the books are suitable for class work or for auditioning with classic material.

Pike, Frank, and Dunn, Thomas G. Scenes and Monologues From the New American Theater. New York: Mentor, 1988. Contains both commercial successes and previously unpublished works. Helpful reference material on playwrights' agents and how to obtain new, relatively unknown plays.

Rudnicki, Stefan. Classical Monologues. 4 Vols. New York: Drama Book Specialists, 1979-82. An excellent body of monologues for classical auditioning material, but limited almost exclusively to Renaissance authors.

Shengold, Nina. _The_ _Actor's_ _Book_ _of_ _Contemporary_
Stage _Monologues_. New York: Penguin, 1988. More
than 150 selections for men and women of all
ages, drawn from well known and obscure playwrights. Interesting interviews with Swoozie
Kurtz, Christopher Durang, Lanford Wilson, and
Tina Howe.

Schewel, Amy, and Smith, Marisa. _The_ _Actor's_ _Book_
_of_ _Movie_ _Monologues._ A fun book for acting
classes with much infrequently-done material.
Young actors will not find many characters
within their range, however, and most of the
selections are "signature pieces" for famous
actors from famous films.

Schulman, Michael, and Mekler, Eva. _Contemporary_
Scenes _for_ _Student_ _Actors_. New York: Penguin,
1980. This paperback contains only scenes. The
first fourteen pages present one of the most
succinct and valuable approaches to scene acting that can be found anywhere.

_____. _The_ _Actor's_
Scenebook, _Volume_ _II._ New York: Bantam, 1988.
Both scenes and monologues are contained in
this book, which also contains a valuable introductory section on creating characters.

B. **HANDBOOKS** **ON** **AUDITION** **TECHNIQUE** **AND** **TRAINING**

Craig, David. _On_ _Performing:_ _A_ _Handbook_ _for_ _Ac-_
tors, _Dancers,_ _Singers_ _On_ _the_ _Musical_ _Stage_.
New York: McGraw-Hill, 1988. America's foremost
musical theatre coach delivers his advice to
actors at all levels of experience. Interviews
with nine successful performers and a brief
history of the American musical theater are
also included.

Ellis, Roger. _A_ _Student_ _Actor's_ _Audition_ _Handbook_.
Chicago: Nelson-Hall, 1985. The definitive text
for preparing stage and musical auditions in
step-by-step fashion. Suitable as a class text
or for individual work. Includes valuable chap-
ters on resumes, interviews, and numerous exercises. Written specifically for young professionals and acting students.

110

Hunt, Gordon. How To Audition. New York: Harper and Row, 1977. Though somewhat dated in its references, it contains numerous comments from working professionals on the auditions process as well as a number of helpful guidelines for young actors.

Shurtleff, Michael. Audition. New York: Walker, 1980. A book for the experienced professional on the Shurtleff approach to auditioning and acting. This is the most widely-used audition book on the market, but it's difficult for young professionals to use on their own without workshop instruction by a Shurtleff-trained coach.

Silver, Fred. Auditioning for the Musical Theatre. New York: Penguin, 1988. Sensible pointers on everything from what to wear to what to sing. Contains a valuable section of 130 possible audition songs.

C. Books on Acting As a Career

Callan, K. The New York Agent Book. Los Angeles: Sweden, 1988 (distributed by Broadway Press, New York). Tips from New York's top agents based on extensive interviews. For beginning and experienced actors.

_____. An Actor's Workbook. Los Angeles: Sweden, 1988 (distributed by Broadway Press, New York). Inside tips from Hollywood agents and casting executives. Valuable discussions of how to evaluate your career and your present agent. Step-by-step procedure for finding the right agent.

_____. How to Sell Yourself As An Actor from New York to Los Angeles (and Everywhere In Between). Los Angeles: Sweden, 1988. A realistic and practical exploration of the various aspects of an acting career. The author tends to regard any-work outside of L.A. and New York as amateurish, but despite this provincial attitude the book is valuable reading for new actors fresh out of school.

Cohen, Robert. Acting Professionally. Third ed.

Palo Alto, California: Mayfield, 1981. The most straightforward, accurate, and honest description of the business of being an actor, by a working professional. "Must" reading for every would-be actor.

Hunt, Cecily. How to Make Money and Get Started in Commercials and Modelling. New York: Van Nostrand Rinehart, 1982. As its title suggests, this is an excellent text for breaking into the commercial aspects of the industry without much experience. Filled with details, necessary facts, up-to-date information and exercises.

Katz, Judith. The Business of Show Business. New York: Harper & Row, 1981. A highly motivational and very readable book which lays out many options open to young actors. Takes much of the dreaded "mystique" away from the profession.

Logan, Tom. How to Act and East At the Same Time. Washington, D.C.: Communications, 1982. Like the Cohen book, "must" reading for young actors breaking into the profession. Up-to-date figures and solid information, but no treatment of acting methods for preparing auditions.

_____. Acting in the Million Dollar Minute: the Art and Business of Performing in TV Commercials. Washington, D.C.: Communications, 1984. Like his other book, this one is also detailed and indispensable reading for anyone considering this aspect of the profession.

McNoughton, Robert and McNoughton, Bruce. Act Now: An Actor's Guide for Breaking-In. Hollywood: Global, 1982. An outstanding up-to-date perspective on stage and film acting which deals especially with young actors.

Moore, Dick. Opportunities in Acting Careers. Lincolnwood, Illinois: National Textbook, 1986. This valuable book is written especially for undergraduate and graduate students. An overview of the many possibilities for using one's collegiate acting training in the entertainment industry.

Rogers, Lynne, and Henry, Marie. How to Be A Working Actor. New York: Evans, 1986. Step-by-step procedures for getting yourself established today. Up-to-date, with a very businesslike approach to marketing yourself, from two women who learned it from the ground up.

CREDITS

M. BUTTERFLY by David Henry Hwang. Copyright © 1989 by
David Henry Hwang. Reprinted by arrangement with NAL
Penguin Inc., New York, New York.

BIG TIME by Keith Reddin. Reprinted by special arrangement with the author, and with Richard P. Kra-
wetz, Agency for the Performing Arts, 888 Seventh
Ave., New York 10106.

THIS ONE THING I DO by Claire Braz-Valentine. Reprinted by special arrangement with the author.

WE AREN'T WHAT YOU THINK WE ARE by Kent R. Brown. Reprinted by permission of the author. WE AREN'T WHAT
YOU THINK WE ARE premiered as part of the play PAGEANT
at the Arkansas Repertory Theatre in January, 1988.
Music and Lyrics by Michael Rice; Book by Jack Heif-
ner, Romulus Linney, Kent R. Brown, Hank Bates, Mary
Rohde, and Cliff Fannin Baker; Direction by Cliff Fannin Baker.

AS IT IS IN HEAVEN by Joe Sutton. Copyright © 1986,
1987 by Joe Sutton. CAUTION: All rights reserved. Except for brief passages quoted in newspaper, magazine,
radio or television review, no part of this book may
be reproduced in any form or by any means, electronic
or mechanical, including photocopying or recording, or
by an information storage and retrieval system, without permission in writing by the author. Professionals
and amateurs are hereby warned that AS IT IS IN HEAVEN
being fully protected under the Copyright Laws of the
United States of America and all other countries of
the Berne and Universal Copyright Convention, is subject to a royalty. All rights including, but not limited to, professional, amateur, recording, motion picture, recitation, lecturing, public reading, radio and
television broadcasting, and the rights of translation
into foreign languages are expressly reserved. Particular emphasis is placed upon the question of readings
and all uses of the play by educational institutions,
permission for which must be secured from the author's
representative: Peter Franklin, William Morris Agency,
1350 Avenue of the Americas, New York, NY 10019; (212)
586-5100.

THE LITTLE TOMMY PARKER CELEBRATED COLORED MINSTREL
SHOW by Carlyle Brown is reprinted by special arrange-

114

115

116

117

cial arrangement with the author.

About the Author

Roger Ellis is an actor, director, and coach who trained in stage and media acting on the west coast and in New York. He has studied and worked with some of the nation's most famous directors, actors, and teachers, and has published three books and numerous articles on the professional stage. For five years he was chairman of the Michigan Theatre Association's Professional Auditions program. He lives in Grand Rapids, Michigan where he is currently on the theatre faculty of Grand Valley State University.